GONDOLIN PRESS

Kiko Argüello

ANNOTATIONS

1988-2014

gondolin press

ANNOTATIONS 1988-2014 – *Kiko Argüello*

Original title: *Anotaciones (1988-2014)*

Translation: Kirsten Dhillon, Pablo & Debora Martinez, Peter Waymel
Revisions: Fr. Manuel Duenas, J.C.L,
Editing: David and Michelle Rak

© gondolin press
1331 Red Cedar Cir
80524 Fort Collins CO

www.gondolinpress.com
info@gondolinpress.com

2018 © Gondolin Institute LLC
Hard cover Book ISBN 978-1-945658-15-0
Soft cover ISBN: 978-1-945658-16-7

All the literary and artistic rights are reserved. The rights for translation, electronic storage, copying and total or partial adaptation, by any equipment, (including microfilm and photostatic copies) are reserved for all countries. The Editor remains at the disposal of any unknown holders of rights who have not been identified.

Printed in USA
First edition: February 2020

"It is necessary to make Christian Communities
like the Holy Family of Nazareth
that live in humility, simplicity and praise;
the other is Christ."

(Words inspired to Kiko Argüello by the Blessed Virgin Mary,
December 8, 1959)

FOREWORD

by Cardinal Sean Patrick O'Malley, OFM Cap.
Archbishop of Boston

Just as in the history of the Church there have been moments when great religious communities sprang up to respond to the needs of the times with charisms that made the Gospel more accessible, more real to God's people, in recent decades the flourishing of so many new ecclesial communities has manifested the presence of the Holy Spirit in the Church. With over 22,000 communities, about 1,500 seminarians and thousands of missionaries sent throughout the world to evangelize, the Neocatechumenal Way has made an enormous impact in the contemporary Church.

Like the Franciscan Order, the Neocatechumenal Way began with the dramatic conversion of the man who was destined to be the instrument of grace that allowed this new reality to be born in the Church. Some of the same things that influenced Kiko Argüello were very important parts of my own vocation, and hence I read these *Annotations* with an insight of how powerful these forces have been in the life of the Church.

As a seminarian I made the Cursillo de Cristiandad. In those days, it was still a Spanish phenomenon, even in the United States. It was so refreshing to see the zeal of lay men and women assuming leadership roles, witnessing to their faith and working to transform the world with the light of the Gospel. Around the same time, Kiko made the Cursillo and was deeply affected by the course in the Catholic faith, taught by lay leaders with a deep sense of community and a desire to build up the body of Christ. The heart of the Cursillo was the theology of grace and the sacramental life of the community with a sense of mission and a zeal to evangelize. In some

Cursillos, the Rollo de Sacramentos could last five or six hours.

Kiko was also very much influenced by the figure of Charles de Foucauld, who sought to lead the "life of Nazareth" in the midst of the poor and marginalized. As a seminarian, I was also very struck by this Lawrence of Arabia who became a modern-day St. Francis, living with the poor and serving them as a universal brother. I was so grateful to my superiors when they allowed me to live among the immigrants that we served and share their physical hardships. It was one of the happiest periods of my life.

Hence, when I read about Kiko going to live in the slums of Madrid, I know what a transformative experience that can be. It is among the poor that we learn to depend on God's love. Kiko cites the beautiful prayer of abandonment that Blessed Charles left us as a gloss on the Our Father and which is an act of complete trust in our loving God.

Francis of Assisi's conversion was occasioned by an encounter with a leper. The young Francis had a terrible repulsion for leprosy and always fled when he saw someone afflicted with this terrible disease. But the grace of God allowed Francis to overcome his spiritual blindness and to find in the leper a neighbor, a brother, a sacrament of Christ. I always say that Francis did not cure the leper, the leper cured him. The leper cured him of his fear, his vanity, his self-centeredness, his blindness to the suffering of others.

Annotations allows us to catch a glimpse of how the poor helped Kiko to discover the real presence of Christ in the least of our brothers and sisters. This modern Francis also had his Clare. Carmen Hernandez helped him on the path to establishing the Way. Carmen was a force of nature, an extraordinary woman who shared Kiko's vision and always challenged him to new heights.

Pope John Paul II in his letter to artists included the quote from Dostoevsky's *The Idiot*: "The world will be saved by beauty." Kiko discovered God not just in the pain and the suffering of the poor and outcast, but also in the beauty of music and art where God's love and beauty are reflected. Kiko's aesthetics have been a crucial element in the spirituality that imbues his followers.

Kiko, like many great believers of the past, embraces the radical message of the Gospel with courage and trust, and strives to build a community like the one described by Luke in the Acts of the Apostles – a community where people are united by the Word of God and the teachings of the Apostles, by fellowship, prayer and by the breaking of the Bread.

Kiko has a sacramental vision that places baptism and the Eucharist at the center of our life as Jesus' disciples. For too many Catholics, baptism has become a folkloric ritual to mark a birth in the family. Kiko uses the Church's liturgy of the Rite of Christian Initiation to mark out a way of conversion, transformation and enlightenment.

The breaking of the Bread – the celebration of the Eucharist – is truly the centerpiece of the life of the Christian community, and this is so evident in the celebrations of the Neocatechumenal Way. Through Word and sacrament, the members of the Way find the strength in a community to embrace the mission that God has given to Christians to be an evangelizing and healing force in the world.

Living our baptism, united and strengthened by the Eucharist and the living witness of the community, allows people to embrace their personal mission, their personal vocation. The vocation to marriage and family is so strong in the Neocatechumenal Way. The openness to life is a great source of encouragement even to other young people not of the Way, who are often fearful of the responsibilities of parenthood.

The courage and generosity of young men and women who offer themselves for priesthood or consecrated life is a powerful witness. The complete availability to be sent to a seminary or a mission in a far-off land manifests the radical call to discipleship that the charism of the Neocatechumenal Way has inspired in so many people.

By placing the Paschal Mystery at the center of the Christian experience, the Neocatechumenal Way has greatly contributed to bringing the teachings of the Second Vatican Council into the life of the parishes where the Way is present. The announcement of the Kerygma as a force for conversion and renewal has changed the lives of many dormant Catholics.

This extraordinary volume, *Annotations* 1988-2014, allows us a glimpse into the soul of the author much like Pascal's *Pensées*, Miguel de Unamuno's *Diario intimo*, or St. Josemaria's *Camino*. This book will be a very important key to understanding Kiko Argüello and the revolution sparked by his conversion that has been an invitation to thousands who, like the Spirit-filled community of the Acts of the Apostles, are of the Way.

PREFACE

by John Garvey
President of the Catholic University of America

The Catholic Church is going through a trial of critical examination unlike anything it has experienced since the Reformation. It was set off by the disclosure of sexual and financial abuse by clergy in a number of countries, including the United States. News of such behavior would unsettle religious convictions even in the most devout society. In an increasingly secular west, it has had still greater impact on people whose attachment to the faith was already frayed by the friction of a hostile culture.

It is natural that the reports of abuse have caused a loss of confidence in the clergy and the episcopacy. Among Catholics who continue to love the Church despite the bad news, there is hope that the laity can play a part in restoring order and confidence. This explains the effort to extend the idea of lay review boards, already used for charges against priests, to cases involving bishops. The same sentiment has brought renewed attention to the roles lay people can fill as deacons, as members of parish councils and finance councils, in chanceries, on school boards, and so on.

These are welcome contributions, and they will help a lot to eliminate bad behavior and prevent a recurrence. But even if they are effective, they won't stem the tide of departures from the Church, nor bring people back to the faith. It's good news that a parish's financial statements are transparent, and children are safe. But that's not *the* Good News.

Vatican II's Dogmatic Constitution on the Church, *Lumen Gentium*, says that the laity "are given this special vocation: to make the Church present and fruitful in those places and circumstances where it is only through them that she can become the salt of the earth." Through their baptism and confirmation, the laity are called to spread the Good News in their families, their workplaces, among their friends, and on street corners.

This is the work the Church's lay movements and new communities are doing. They are not concerned with addressing the current crises of personnel and finance. Rather, they devote their efforts to preaching what draws people to the Church — God's love and mercy. Their work is bringing to life the ambitions of the Second Vatican Council.

At The Catholic University of America, we have tried to recognize the importance of this work by giving honorary degrees to the leaders of the movements and new communities — Andrea Riccardi, the founder of Sant' Egidio; Chiara Lubich, the founder of Focolare; Fr. Julián Carrón, the leader of Communion and Liberation. Among these lay movements, none has been more attractive and influential than the Neocatechumenal Way. At our 2015 commencement, we gave honorary degrees to Kiko Argüello and Carmen Hernández, initiators of the Way.

Since its beginning in Madrid in 1964, the Way has attracted more than a million adherents around the world. They include two of my sisters and their spouses, and more than a dozen of my nieces and nephews. One of my godchildren is a priest in the Way; another is serving a *missio ad gentes* in Brooklyn. I have attended World Youth Days in Madrid, in Krakow, in Rio with hundreds of thousands of young people from the Way, drawn by the opportunity to meet the Holy Father.

Kiko's reflections collected in this book help to explain why the Way has appealed to so many people. One can't help but be impressed by the sheer immensity of the effort he and Carmen expended over more than fifty years. The *Annotations* were jotted down over only about half that period. But they show Kiko visiting six continents and scores of countries to preach the gospel.

The Way began as an outreach to social outcasts. It continues to have a special appeal for people who have encountered difficulty in their lives. Its message, the message of the gospel, is that Christ loves us despite our sins. Perhaps his roots in this soil have taught Kiko the lesson of humility. He begins the book by saying that "everything in which God dwells is humble" (5). This outreach may also explain why humble people are drawn to Kiko. Because "[h]e who is humble does not take account of evil, he understands it" (28).

Like Communion and Liberation, the Neocatechumenal Way puts a particular emphasis on the way beauty draws us to God. This is as true for the poor and humble as it is for others. As Kiko says, "We can lack many things, but not beauty. In it we realize that 'someone' *wants us to fall in love with him*" (298). Many of the songs sung in the celebrations and liturgies of the Way are his compositions. I have visited the Redemptoris Mater seminaries in Denver and Newark where his architectural designs are evident. In these *Annotations* we see him painting the churches of St. Frances Cabrini in Rome (174) and St. Bartholomew in Tuto in Florence (226). We see him saying how hurt he was by the criticism of his paintings in the cathedral apse in Madrid (386). However just the professional reception of his artistic works might be, there can be no quarrel with his instinct. "The beauty of all that surrounds us in nature is a mirror of the love that God has for mankind" (378).

If the laity are to play their proper part in spreading the gospel through the movements and new communities that have come to life since Vatican II, it is essential that they themselves be properly catechized. This is a particular strength of the Way. Kiko stresses that "The Way is supported by three things: Word, Liturgy, and... Community" (315). The catechumenate is by definition an itinerary of Christian initiation. This is not a simple and enthusiastic movement. It is a lifelong education in the faith.

The most striking thing about the *Annotations*, though, is not the view it offers of the progress of the Way, nor the humility of its founder, nor the emphasis on beauty and the gospel. It is the feeling the reader gets of eavesdropping on a conversation the writer is having with God. This is not a third person account. It speaks to God in the second person, like the Psalms. ("O Lord, how many are my foes!" "My God my God, why hast thou forsaken me?") We hear, or overhear, Kiko saying, "Lord, you are so wonderful that the thought of you, looking at you, makes me ashamed; I, who am such a sinner. You love me so much. Blessed be You, Lord!" (41).

That makes it a good book to pray with. What better invitation can there be to a life of faith?

INTRODUCTION

For almost thirty years, I have been writing in notebooks in a sporadic and irregular manner – and without any definite intention – some thoughts, reflections, maxims,[1] memories, considerations, notes, soliloquies, prayers, etc. that have arisen within me during the mission of evangelization and catechesis to which the Lord called me in the Church, along with Carmen Hernandez and Fr. Mario Pezzi.

From time to time, the thought of publishing these notes crossed my mind. I rejected this out of caution and for fear that it might be only ambition, born of my vanity.

Now that I am publishing these annotations – because I was asked earnestly to do so – I remember once more what that elderly priest once told me, "Never avoid doing good for fear of vanity, because this comes from the devil."

What is the good in this case? To proclaim the glory of God, giving witness to his gratuitous love and his unconditional faithfulness to me who, as will be seen, am inadequate, unworthy, useless, unfaithful…

If these annotations help someone, blessed be God. My hope is that the reader, through the intercession of the Blessed Virgin Mary, who inspired and guides the Neocatechumenal Way, may commend me to the mercy of our Lord Jesus Christ, so that I may be saved.

Pray for me, for I am a sinner.

---

[1] Some of the maxims are inspired by the Bible, the writings of the saints, the sayings of the Desert Fathers and the Talmud.

With gratitude to the Holy Fathers
St. Paul VI
John Paul I
St. John Paul II
Benedict XVI
and Pope Francis
who in their Petrine ministry have recognized,
approved, confirmed and supported
the Neocatechumenal Way
as an itinerary of Christian initiation
and permanent formation in faith
as a fruit of the Council.

Kiko Argüello

ANNOTATIONS
1988-2014

1. What does it mean to be Christian? To have discernment.

2. How is discernment attained? Through fear.

3. What is fear? To expect at every moment to fall into disgrace and to say to yourself, "Why does this happen to others and not to me? I am not better than them."

4. What is humility? To be, above all, one in the One.

5. Everything in which God dwells is humble.

6. All of creation is full of humility, because it is full of obedience.

7. Remember, my child, that purity and chastity are honored on earth and in heaven.

8. You must learn to despoil yourself of everything periodically, so that you may be freer and happier.

9. Ascend to God by descending the stairs of humility.

10. Being humble makes the Christian great.

11. What is it that attracts us to nature? Its perfection? Its strength? Its beauty? Its quietness? Its humility and obedience. We long for these because we lack them. They *speak to us of God.*

12. Remember, my child, that before and above all else you need humility, for it defeats the adversary and destroys everything that comes from the enemy.

13. In your relationships with others, never let asking for forgiveness be far from your lips. This keeps the devil's snares at bay.

14. Remember, you who are preparing yourself to become a priest of the holy Church of God, that you will be the minister of a new worship, of a new covenant, of a new sanctuary purified by the blood of God Himself. Christ confirms, seals, blesses and makes the new reality present through you. He lives in you and for you. He has already sanctified, taught, and healed; you give him freely, you minister to him today, making everyone praise Christ.
Christ does not give you a worldly kind of power, but rather the capacity for a service, for his service. This service is fundamentally sacramental. Christ acts and lives in history through you and the whole Church. You are to the Church what the head is to

the body: a head alone, without a body, cannot exist; it does not exist and has no meaning. You are placed over the body; it is the body that carries you, that moves. Always move together with your body: you are not alone.

You signify, you make present, you "create", the new eschatological reality where the Risen Christ is.

15. "If you want to be perfect, go, sell your goods, then come and follow me."[2]

16. Remember, my child, that the only happiness in this world is to love God; everything else is vanity.

17. To love you, my Lord, is true happiness.

18. Oh, how painful my life is with my sins, without You! And the beauty of You and of your love, and walking toward death… toward You.

19. "The Lord said, 'I thirst.' And they gave him vinegar to drink."[3] His blood flowed to pay for our sins, and his thirst grew. Our lack of love; thirst for love… "Give me to drink,"[4] said Jesus to the Samaritan woman. "Can you drink the cup that I will drink…?"[5] And the psalm says, "they gave me

---

[2] Cf. Mt 19:21.
[3] Cf. Jn 19:28-29.
[4] Jn 4:7.
[5] Mt 20:22.

vinegar to drink when I was thirsty."[6] "A jar full of sour wine stood there; so, putting a sponge soaked in the wine on a hyssop stick, they held it up to his mouth. After Jesus had taken the wine he said, 'It is fulfilled': and bowing his head he gave up his spirit."[7] "Blessed are those who hunger and thirst for uprightness: they shall have their fill."[8] "Oh, come to the water all of you who are thirsty...!"[9] "Wisdom has... mixed her wine, laid her table..." "Come and eat..., drink the wine that I have mixed.'"[10]

My Jesus, you thirst for my love. If I stop sinning, I satisfy your thirst. My sins make You bleed to death; as they do to me, like the hemorrhaging woman.[11] And they make you thirst, a terrible thirst. May I stop making your blood run. May I be able to quench your thirst. May I be able to love you.

20. My total weakness astounds me. Lord Jesus, have pity on me! Do not allow me to become conceited. I am a miserable person and You fill me with your grace, your tenderness, your love and mercy. To follow your footprints. From grace to grace, from gift to gift, from surprise to surprise, and your love,

---

[6] Ps 69:21.
[7] Jn 19:29-30.
[8] Mt 5:6.
[9] Is 55:1.
[10] Prov 9:1-2,5.
[11] Mk 5:25-34.

your wonderful love, and I...ungrateful, a sinner. Help me, Lord!

21. I will shout: Papa! *Abba!*[12] And I will take refuge in You.

22. You drew close to me and I crucified You. You did not resist evil,[13] did not escape, continued loving me, wanted to enter into me. I killed You when your "I" became a "You". You offered yourself for me, a murderer, and God the Father accepted your offering and resurrected You. He forgave me and you made me one flesh with You forever.[14] The love that I never knew appeared.
I live, but it is not I but You who live with me, in me.[15] I have known love, to pass to the other person. You have opened a way through death so that I might become you with my neighbor. You give me your victory over death, you give me your Spirit. You give me Yourself: love.
The other always crucifies me with his otherness: I can take on that which I am not, even though it destroys me. Can I make it my own by dying? I am able to not resist evil. I am able to love the enemy.[16]

---

[12] Cf. Rom 8:15.
[13] Cf. Mt 5:39.
[14] Cf. Eph 5:31-32.
[15] Cf. Gal 2:20.
[16] Cf. Mt 5:39,44.

23. I am able to love as *You* have loved me…[17] I am able to be a Christian.

    Every mortification, small or great, which You have invited me to sow in myself, with your grace, has always born fruit.

24. I am a despicable and hypocritical being; like a clown, many times I preach things I do not do… Nothing matters to me without your love. You love me and that's enough for me. My weaknesses, my deepest imperfections, make me suffer so much. But the memory of your love, seeing you crucified for me, moves me, overwhelms me, makes me cry. Oh, Jesus, my Lord, to love you, to desire you, to be in You…! Come! Help me, let us go together, let us die, the two of us. In You alone I feel love for the others and, if I separate myself from You, so many times I detest them. In You men become one. I am moved by their miseries and sufferings, and I think… if they knew your love… Thousands and thousands of vagabonds, poor people, miserable people, crawling, searching through the trash of the great cities… Criminal Babylon.[18] Walking shadows, resigned to an existence that leads them to an inertia that, little by little, comes to a halt and, full of wounds, drunk, dirty, thrown out into the streets, they die at our feet without knowing love, your love. They bear your image, they bear You

---

[17] Cf. Jn 13:34.
[18] Ps 137:8.

without knowing it. You were thrown out of the city, taken out of it like trash that is thrown out, like the scapegoat that was led out, loaded with the sins of the people.[19] Whoever led it out became impure, so stained was he by it.[20] It was terrifying to think that it bore all the sins of the people. It could not remain in the city. Its place was with the demons. And there, in the desert, it was abandoned to the wild beasts and to death.

25. Lord Jesus, you love me so much that it makes me ashamed.

26. He who is *humble is obedient*.

27. He who is humble forgives before they ask him for forgiveness.

28. He who is humble does not take account of evil,[21] he understands it.

29. He who is humble knows the traps of the enemy and knows that at any moment we are capable of judging, of being jealous, of thinking badly... that is why he excuses everything.[22]

30. Without humility, one cannot obtain discernment.

---

[19] Cf. Lev 16:21.
[20] Cf. Lev 16:26.
[21] Cf. 1 Cor 13: 5.
[22] Cf. 1 Cor 13:7.

31. Psalm
To bless you, Lord,
and from within,
in the tenderness of your love,
immersed in the flow of my pen, to sing,
in the gliding of my fingers, to write.
What is my being,
that You hold with your love,
that struggles between nothingness and fear
of the abyss, of horror,
of a cruelty that knows no end…
I am in You and it could be otherwise.
I am in You, in the wonder of your gracious love.
I am, I am begotten,
I am constantly,
and it could be otherwise.
I am a constant wonder.
I am an endless succession of instants,
endlessly occurring in real time.
To be and not to be.
I am conscious that we can only be in You,
why haven't I been?
The more I am in your love,
the more painful is the fear of not being,
of the possibility of not being,
of the fear of ceasing to be,
of the hell of losing You.
How subtle, how fragile is
the tenuous fabric of my being,
that the breeze of your love moves.
From within,

from the depths of my being,
in the infinite cosmos of my being,
You love me and I am.
"And God said, 'Let there be light.'"[23]
To bless you, Lord,
and from within,
in the tenderness of your love,
enveloped always in your humility,
in fear.
Come!
Why are we terrified by what is free?
Because we cannot dominate it,
because it is and it could not be…
Above this grace, your love,
which gives me my being from You.
And I almost die
thinking and feeling
the cries and groans of that hell
from which you draw me out every day.
"You are my son, today have I begotten you".[24]
My Jesus, help me to carry your love
in this constant precariousness
of being and not being in You,
of grace and sin.
Give me your Spirit
that imprints your essence in me,
that brands me, that burns me,

---

[23] Cf. Gn 1:3.
[24] Cf. Ps 2:7.

that I might desire forever: You.[25]
"Father… may the Spirit (love)
with which you have loved me
be in them and I in them."[26]
This is how Jesus prays.
That your love, Father, may be in me
and He, Jesus, in me.
The love with which You, Father,
have loved Jesus. Love.
"I have made your Name known to them…"[27]
You make known to us the person *of the Father,*
so that the love with which the Father loves us
may be in us.
The Father loves us
to the point of handing over his only Son to death,
to pain, to terror, to Hell…
so that I might be saved from all of that,
might be his son,
might live eternally,
so that I might know the love of the Father
and it may live in me forever.
And this infinite love,
which can no longer be separated from me,[28]
is in the Son totally,
who assumes it, obeys it and is crucified for me,
so that he may be one *in me.*

---

[25] Cf. 2 Cor 3:17.
[26] Cf. Jn 17:26.
[27] Ibid.
[28] Cf. Rom 8:35-39.

and the world may believe in this love.[29]
God's love,
divine love that erupts in the world
and creates the one, holy, and Catholic Church.
For everyone, universal.
One with the Father,
one with the Son,
one in the Spirit of holiness.
Holy Spirit,
holy because He loves us,
we, who are sinners.
Amen.

32. When they persecute you, my child, remember that it is better to be persecuted than to persecute. When they humiliate you, remember that it is better to be humiliated than to humiliate. And rejoice.[30]

33. The beginning of conversion is to consider oneself a sinner.

34. If every moment you try to do God's will, you will be happy, everything will turn out well for you.[31]

35. The will of God is for you to be holy.[32] The will of God is holy. God is holy.[33]

---

[29] Cf. Jn 17:21.
[30] Cf. *Talmud, Tractate Baba Kamma*, Chapter VIII and Mt 5:11-12.
[31] Cf. Ps 1:3.
[32] Cf. 1 Thes 4:3.
[33] Cf. Lev 19:2.

36. Lord, You are in my history. "I am who am," (who will be, who will stay...)[34]. You are the One who stays. How many wonders, how much love, how many trials in which You have appeared, saving. The perfection of history... The prophecy of the Word fulfilled: let it be done as it is written. Your Word makes history, saves it, and in it we are Yours.

37. I have seen every word I have read in the Scriptures fulfilled. That's why they are the fountain of faith and hope.

38. To scrutinize the Scriptures is to know of your love and my history.

39. In your book it is written of me to do your will, Lord. Here I am.[35]

40. We must accept the fact that Christ is the Servant of Yahweh, the suffering Servant that takes upon himself the sins of humanity.[36] The Church, which has encountered him risen, gives him to the world, through the *littleness* of the preaching;[37] This one, who for a little while we see burdened with ignominy, will return on the clouds of the air as the "Son of man" with power and glory.[38]

---

[34] Cf. Ex 3:14.
[35] Cf. Ps 40:7-8; Heb. 10:7.
[36] Cf. Is 53:4.
[37] Cf. 1 Cor 1:18.
[38] Cf. Mt 24:30.

We must carry his weakness and ignominy, completing in our body what is lacking in his passion for this generation.[39] Let us resist the temptation of power, because it is the weakness of God that converts us, which saves the world. We preach Christ, and Christ crucified.[40] Meanwhile men devour and kill each other... The Church bears their sins with Christ on the cross, she doesn't destroy them with the sword. Although at times the totalitarian temptation is very strong, it's always a betrayal, it's always a temptation. Christ died unarmed on a cross, without judging, excusing. Those who have received his Spirit always do the same. Let us not allow ourselves to be deceived.

41. Lord, you are so wonderful that the thought of you, looking at you, makes me ashamed; I, who am such a sinner. You love me so much. Blessed be You, Lord!

42. How can I love the Lord with all my heart, with all my soul and with all my strength?[41]
With all your heart: accepting, without grumbling against God, the sufferings, the discomforts of your situation (lack of sleep, tiredness, sickness, conflicts with the one with whom you walk, misunderstandings...), and fasting.

---

[39] Cf. Col 1:24.
[40] Cf. 1 Cor 1:23.
[41] Cf. Dt 6:5; Mk 12:30.

With all your soul, or your mind: accepting the cross that crucifies the depths of your ego (humiliations, destruction of your works and projects, failures…), and praying.

With all your strength: putting all your work at the service of the Lord, and giving alms, accepting total precariousness in order to be free.

43. And how can I love my neighbor as myself?[42] *By considering him superior to yourself.*[43] Above all, the poor, those who suffer sicknesses or are victims of some terrible vice: drugs, lust, alcoholism, etc. Remaining in the truth about yourself: that you are a sinner.

44. Remember, my child, that you don't heal weakness. God has wished to deposit an infinite treasure in an earthen vessel.[44] Let us be careful not to break it by striking it with sin, losing in this way the holiness of God, its precious content.

45. Being aware of your own weakness will make you strong.

46. He who knows that he is weak is strong. And he who believes himself to be strong is weak.

---

[42] Cf. Lev 19:18; Mk 12:31.
[43] Cf. Phil 2:3.
[44] Cf. 2 Cor 4:7.

47. The one who knows his weakness has self-discernment. If the potter's jar is knocked against iron, it breaks.

48. If we were not weak, we would not be able to evangelize: we would preach ourselves.[45]

49. Accept your reality and you will understand the goodness and love of God.

50. He who does not accept his weakness is proud and lazy: he does not want to go on fighting.

51. Remember that to be Christian means to start anew every day.

52. God gives you his grace for each day. Every day he gives you the bread you need to be holy that day.[46] If you worry about the future or think about tomorrow,[47] this comes from you, you are disobeying and you already have your punishment: anxiety. You are a proud person who does not accept to be dependent on someone else; you don't know how to obey; you don't love. Only he who obeys loves.

53. "Father, I have fallen."
    "Get up."

---

[45] Cf. 2 Cor 4:5; 10:12.
[46] Cf. Mt 6:11.
[47] Cf. Mt 6:34.

"Father, I fell again."
"Get up again."
"For how long?"
"Until death finds you fallen or standing. If it finds you fallen, you will be condemned; if it finds you standing, you will be saved."[48]

54. The righteous man sins seven times and rises again seven times.[49]

55. Do not judge.[50] If you judge, it is because you are not humble. If you are not humble, you do not have true peace. If you do not have true peace, you suffer. If you suffer, you need to gratify yourself by sinning. If you sin, you kill yourself.[51] He who kills himself, condemns himself. Do not judge…

56. He who judges, kills.

57. Are you a sinner? I, personally, am not scandalized. I love you; I understand you. I am no better than you. It is you who are scandalized of yourself; you don't understand yourself, and that is because you believe you are better than others… Courage, God loves you. Get up. Begin again. Ask for forgiveness.

---

[48] Cf. *Sayings of the Desert Fathers* in *PL 73:1034*.
[49] Cf. Prov 24:16.
[50] Mt 7:1.
[51] Cf. James 1:15.

58. Woe is me, I who am the most miserable of all men! I make others run while I am about to be disqualified.[52] I do not punish my body.[53] Gluttony, impurity, avarice and such a lack of humility, fill my itinerant catechist knapsack. I speak and don't do what I say;[54] I preach but I don't practice. Who will be able to save me after the miracles and countless marvels done for us? I am ungrateful. Lord, have mercy!

    You allow this, to bring down my pride, so that I may touch, experience and see what I am: worse than the others! To accept myself this way and suffer the humiliation and terror of being condemned… To preach while feeling unworthy… and to trust in you who love me, accept me, put up with me, forgive me a thousand and one times a day. You are wonderful, and I… What does it matter? What matters is You, and your love, your immense love, You, the "Lover of Mankind."[55]

59. If you only knew how much God loves you, you would be happy. What is it that prevents you from seeing his love?

60. I am a wretch. You correct me and you love me. Blessed be your name, Lord.

---

[52] Cf. 1 Cor 9:27.
[53] Cf. ibid.
[54] Cf. Mt 23:3.
[55] Cf. Ws 7:23.

61. Grant me, Lord, to love my enemies, and not resist evil.[56] Grant me your tenderness, your immense humility. You always encourage me, from within, you never judge me, you love me, you say to me, "Courage!"

62. Tenderness toward my enemies: they do me the immense good of making me resemble Christ. Ineffable mystery of the love of God: enemies, hostility, conspiracy, calumny…how difficult. My God, you carried their sins upon yourself, holy Lamb.[57] And I? How difficult. Everything hurts me. I am too sensitive, a useless servant.[58] Help me!

63. My son, love Christ above everyone and everything. Give yourself to Him, become one with Him, one flesh.[59] Live with Him, from Him and for Him, and thousands and thousands around you will find salvation.

64. He will give you his peace, he will give you that strength and freedom that you truly desire. He will give you the grace to accept your weakness. He will make you happy.

---

[56] Cf. Mt 5:39, 44.
[57] Cf. Jn 1:29.
[58] Cf. Lk 17:10.
[59] Cf. Eph 5:31-32.

65. The head and members form one body.[60] Christ, our head,[61] took upon himself the sins of all. In each generation, his members make this visible and bring it to fulfillment in his body: love for one's enemy, Christian love, "heavenly agape." A single spirit, head and members, permeates the body, animates it, gives it life. Head and members show the love of God for mankind; they make it sacramentally visible, they give salvation.

66. To take sins away, to forgive sins. Sin dwells in man[62] inciting his members to place themselves at his service, at the service of his own pleasure, his comfort, his whims, to make himself the only one in everything. Everything has to be for him; *he offers everything* to himself:[63] his neighbor exists for him. Sin enslaves him, tyrannizes him from within, makes demands on him and tells him, "You are god." Sin makes the life of man miserable. Man cannot take away his sins by himself. But he can ask for forgiveness and for help.

67. The man in whose flesh sin abides does not obey God, nor can he, says St. Paul.[64] Because sin consists of the fact that he has killed the Word

---

[60] Cf. 1 Cor 12:12.
[61] Cf. Eph 1:22.
[62] Cf. Rom 7:20.
[63] Cf. 2 Cor 5:18.
[64] Cf. Rom 8:7.

within him, in whom he was created,[65] and has made himself god. If he would obey, if he could obey, he would no longer be a slave to sin.[66] One obeys a superior... But he cannot. He needs to meet Christ who took upon himself our sins, who killed sin in the flesh, in our flesh.[67] He took away all of its trophies, he left it with nothing. He took the law and fulfilled it in his flesh. Christ took our flesh and brought it to humility, submerged our members in a bath of *kenosis*,[68] of love for the other. He died for me.

68. "*Shema*, Israel. Listen: God is one, He is the only one; you will love God with all your heart, with all your soul, with all your strength..."[69] On the cross, the heart of Jesus is pierced; his soul, his mind, is crowned with thorns; his strength – his hands and feet – are nailed to the wood. "Cursed be the one who hangs from a tree."[70] He hangs from the wood of the cross and he makes himself cursed in our place, for us, loving us more than himself.

St. Paul says that the devil, taking occasion of the law, seduced us and killed us.[71] That is, the devil tells us that God gave us the *Torah* to limit us, to

---

[65] Cf. Jn 1:3; Col. 1:16.
[66] Cf. Jn 8:34.
[67] Cf. Rom. 8:3.
[68] Cf. Phil 2:7.
[69] Cf. Dt 6:4-5; Mk 12:30.
[70] Cf. Gal 3:13.
[71] Cf. Rom 7:11.

"castrate" us, because, ultimately, he is jealous, he hates us and doesn't want us to be gods; that's why he gave us the Tablets. The devil invites us to break the Tablets, to be libertines, to sin, to kill God inside us, not to obey; he deceives us, seduces us, showing us a false freedom, a deceitful way of being free or being adults. He creates a selfish nucleus within us. He places our ego at the center of the universe, and incites us, by flattering us, to demand that time, history, the cosmos, and people submit to our ego. If they do not do so, he prompts us to judge, to rebel, to demand, to kill, to yell, to destroy, to make war.

Our members have been robbed by the devil and we have put them at the service of iniquity, of our ego, taking the place of God. To hate, because they do not love me. To judge everyone and everything, because they are not as I say. To kill, when I see that the others are my enemies who want to destroy me. To envy, to fornicate, to possess, to command, to have money, a lot of money… And death? Fear of death,[72] fear of suffering.

69. In every event, whether big or small, that makes you suffer, don't blame anyone, rather think that it comes from the Lord so that you turn your gaze toward Him, so that you pray to Him. It will help you. This has happened to you because of your sins.

---

[72] Cf. Heb 2:15.

70. What does it mean to have humility? To do good to those who have done evil to you.[73]

71. What does it mean to have humility? To accept it, when the other yells at you, thinking that God allows it because he wants to make you holy, and to accept in this way everything that goes against you.

72. Faced with my anguishes, fears and anxieties, the Word of the Lord, "Do not resist evil" always gives me peace. Help me, Lord, not to resist evil, to be Christian.

73. Pieve di Cadore,[74] July 11, 1989.
And the flags were raised all at once,
the standards of that army.
Thousands of voices shouted
and above the clouds the sun appeared.
That little Virgin
and St. James, the pilgrim.
A thousand young people standing,
an army of poor ones.
The voices as one,
the flags
and the standards as one.
St. James, the little Virgin
and a thousand beautiful young people on their feet
offering their faces.

---

[73] Cf. Lk 6:27.
[74] Town in northern Italy.

74. Progress in the way of faith means to be more and more humble, until one arrives at adult faith, which is to consider others superior to yourself.[75]

75. You always repay my evil with goodness. Blessed be your name, Lord. Your holiness, your goodness, your humility, your meekness, your infinite love, full of tenderness... and I, a miserable, perverse and ungrateful being. Help me to love you, to be meek, humble, patient, to return good for evil.

76. Only humility allows us to see, from its 'height', the grace and the reason for certain things that happen to us.

77. In the constant relationship with our Lord Jesus, I always learn from Him to answer evil with good. But afterward...how few times I do it...

78. What is prayer? The Christian's combat.

79. The one who is humble only rarely gets angry.

80. The Lord loves me totally, infinitely... that is enough.

81. Do not resist evil.[76] How can they offend you when they insult you? They reproduce Christ insulted in

---

[75] Cf. Phil 2:3.
[76] Cf. Mt 5:39.

you. Let evil and sin reach you. There is no greater grace on earth.

Only in the cross of Christ does one find perfect happiness, total freedom, love for God and neighbor. Climb up on the cross, carry with Christ the sins of the others, and you will be happy. If you can do that, it has been granted to you from heaven to be Christian, to have the nature of God, to love as God loves, to be a child of God. If you can love like that, you will never die. If you love like that, it means that the Holy Spirit has been given to you. You have the very Spirit of God.

That is the reality of the eternal things the Church gives us through the sacraments. Christ risen from death makes us partakers in his very Spirit, victorious over death, He places his immortal life in us. New creation, children of God, holy, friends of God, heirs of heaven, co-heirs with Christ[77] of his glory, humble, patient, deeply sweet, without judgments, full of compassion toward those who are far away from God and who, therefore, lack heavenly goods. Conquerors of death, we possess a new life within: eternal life, the life of God. It guides us like a light in the midst of a dark sea, in a storm: our boat rises and falls amid the waves, the wind, the rain, the darkness and, before us, the light of the lighthouse of faith, of the divine life in us that encourages us, that makes us walk, that

---

[77] Rom. 8:17.

sustains us with the certainty of the Father's love. It is the participation in the love of the Holy Trinity. The Holy Spirit in us makes us one with the Father and with the Son. Certain of the Father's love, by means of the crucified Son, we possess the Spirit of the promise, which creates us, which recreates us, which lifts us up, which defends us, which testifies to us of the Father and the Son. He himself is the witness *par excellence*; without Him we are nothing. He himself is God.

82. I will glory in my weakness.[78] It shows your existence, Lord, your love and your mercy. In my weakness, your glory appears.

83. My Jesus! You have crucified evil and sin, you have carried them upon yourself without rebelling and have been raised on the cross for us, the world and history, in order to destroy the work of sin. Once sin was crucified, you killed death by your resurrection.

    Sin operates in the world, breaking the relationship of obedience, of love, with God. Sin kills the image of God in us, that is, it kills Christ, the imprint of the divine substance,[79] and it kills us. Sin lives in man's flesh and enslaves him with its demands for power, for being the first, for being loved, for being god, it drives people to drink, to judge, to kill each

---

[78] Cf. 2 Cor 12:9.
[79] Cf. Heb 1:3.

other, to desire to escape from all suffering, to envy, to possess… It blinds men and makes them pursue ephemeral things that give nothing.

Pride, haughtiness, love of money, lust, anger, envy, gluttony… lack of humility… Blind and conceited, man groans trying to gratify himself to quench his thirst: the lack of meaning, and life that flees him, and total weakness and sicknesses and the fear of dying…

My Jesus! You have crucified evil and sin; You have killed death. You have risen from the dead and you give yourself completely to man in the Holy Spirit for a new life, to know humility and tenderness, the sweetness of your love, to stop demanding, to enter into the gratuity of your mercy… to be eternally in You, free, in love, and happy. To You, glory and honor forever. Amen.

84. Who is Jesus Christ? He who has crucified sin and has killed death.[80] The Son of God. "True God from true God. Begotten, not made, consubstantial with the Father… For us men and for our salvation He came down from heaven."[81] He was born in a humble village and of the Blessed Virgin Mary by the work of the Holy Spirit.

---

[80] Cf. *Sayings of the Desert Fathers.*
[81] Cf. *Nicene Creed.*

85. Remember, my son, that if your true, deep, interior work is to obey God and to do his will – one act of obedience after another – then God will obey you.[82]

86. When you see a dog, think: it's better than I, because it's full of affection for people and doesn't judge.[83] I, on the other hand, do not love anyone and am always judging.

87. A fool is one to whom no one can say anything, like Nabal.[84] Do not rebuke a fool, because he will hate you.[85]

88. You are a priest not because of what you have learned, but because of what you have received.

89. Whoever does not obey, does not love. To obey everyone: children, wife, husband, co-workers and friends… To obey is to donate oneself, it is to die to oneself, it is… to be free.

90. Make yourself a slave, and you will be free.

91. Every day, let yourself be killed by the will of others and you will be free.

---

[82] Cf. *Sayings of the Desert Fathers*.
[83] Cf. *Sayings of the Desert Fathers*.
[84] Cf. 1 Sam 25:17.
[85] Cf. Prov. 9:8.

92. What do your opinion, your house, your things, your money matter? Give everything up, every minute, and you will be free.

93. Your wife, your children, your job, your house, your ideas, your plans, your car... all that, what is it? Look at Christ crucified and let others yell at you; accept everything and be free.

94. To love is to obey; to love is to give oneself; to love is to be a lamb led to the slaughter every day,[86] in every moment. To love is to be in God.... To love is to be free.

95. Clothe yourself in grass; sleep on grass; eat grass; make yourself a heart of *iron* and be free... because Christ crucified himself for you.[87]

96. Nothing matters. God alone is enough.[88]

97. If you believe that Christ crucified is God and you act by crucifying yourself in your everyday life, as the truth of love for you, congratulations! You are among the few who are free and happy.

98. The *Book of Psalms* is a ritual of holiness. It is the ritual of the liturgy of life, the highest liturgy: the

---

[86] Jer 11:19; Acts 8:32; Rom 8:36.
[87] Cf. *Sayings of the Desert Fathers*.
[88] Cf. *Poem* by St. Teresa of Jesus.

life of Christ is a holy liturgy that gives us love for God and men.

99. The life of our Lord Jesus is a song, a liturgy, whose ritual is the *Psalter*. To live doing the will of God is to officiate at that liturgy in which the world, time, and things are redeemed in Christ.

100. Sin, living in us,[89] *obliges us* to offer the world and everything and everyone in it to ourselves. A satanic liturgy centered on selfishness: our own ego, the well-being of our ego. The ego, taking the place of God, makes itself tyrannical, cruel, intransigent, scathing, a murderer, a liar... Caught by the demons in a state of dissatisfaction and need, it falls into a thousand traps, in the constant desire for well-being. The demons invite the self to have recourse to magic, astrology, gambling, to commit crimes for money, they make the self believe that everyone is like him, that everyone constantly seeks pleasure at the expense of others, that this is life... the desire for money, lust, death. The soul is dead. Its personhood is dead. Fear of death.[90] Total paganism. Taking refuge in work as the only redemption? They are dead without knowing it. From the perspective of their paganism, escaping from death constantly, the Church seems to be a demand, a law, a moral oppressor. Sin doesn't exist

---

[89] Cf. Rom 7:17.
[90] Cf. Heb 2:15.

– they say – let us eat and drink,[91] let us run in search of pleasure... To satisfy nature, to live. That's how they think, and God loves them nonetheless, and they can be saved.

To evangelize, take them out of slavery to the devil, out of darkness, to the light of the love that God has for them. We can live without offering ourselves everything and everyone. We can live worshipping God our Father, putting ourselves at his service. We can be resurrected with Christ to live a new life in Christ. The "You" of God lives in us, becomes one with my "I". The "You" of God in me is Christ. To him be glory forever. Amen.

101. To be holy living each day in the "I" of Christ, in his constant remembrance, in the constant remembrance of his love, his tenderness, his cross for me.

He is the only one who is never scandalized by me, by my weakness, my misery, my intransigence, my lust, by the multitude of faults and sins that besiege me. Jesus, my beloved, you always say to me, "Courage! I love you!" He has held me tight and doesn't let me go. In His grasp, will I reach heaven...?

I already live in the heaven of his love. I hope not to fall into the hell of myself, to sin mortally, to kill God in me, to despise his Church.... Help me,

---

[91] Cf. 1 Cor 15:32.

Lord. Look at your blessed Mother, who prays for me.

102. He who does only what he wants is a slave to his appetite; he is not free.

103. Not being able to love makes us sad. He who can only do his own will is not free, is not happy. To love is to give oneself to another, to give oneself totally; it is to give one's own self, to give one's own will.

104. Give your own self to Christ and He will distribute it among men; he will multiply it and satisfy multitudes with you: you will be free.

105. Only the one who makes himself a slave of God is *free*.

106. A gentle and light yoke is the yoke (love) of the Lord.[92] It is full of understanding and mercy toward our continuous offenses, full of tenderness and fidelity, of *infinite compassion*, of love without limits. It always forgives, always believes, always hopes, understands everything. Excuses everything.[93] His goodness spreads like a perfume, inundating everything. I feel constantly his holiness in me, his

---

[92] Cf. Mt 11:30.
[93] Cf. 1 Cor 13:7.

love, his tenderness, his compassion, and I see my wickedness, my weakness, my negligence…
To love you, Lord! My life is a mystery. You have fallen in love with me; you have filled me with gifts, and I… Have pity on me lest I be lost!

107. *To live is to navigate*
in the fear of perishing.
To live is to be
in the Other who saves you.
To live is to know
the love of God
that begets you
in a succession
of uninterrupted
instants
of love…
in a cascade
of graces
that invade the world.
To live is to see
in everything that exists
the reflection of God's love
made manifest in Christ.

108. Oh, holy humility of Christ, who can find you, who can possess you, make you one's own, who can espouse you! Holy humility of the heart of Christ, sweet love, gentle repose, you do not resist evil,[94]

---

[94] Cf. Mt 5:39.

you excuse everything, bear everything, believe everything.[95] You are the luminous garment of the true Christian, you are the eternal sweetness of the crucified Lord. Oh, holy humility of Christ…who could find you!

109. There is nothing on earth higher than humility.

110. There is nothing on earth greater than humility.

111. What is humility? The Truth.[96]

112. Where there is humility, there is mercy.

113. The work of a Christian, his everyday task, is conversion.

114. Only humility brings us into the Kingdom of God; it makes us children.[97]

115. Despise everything and you will have discernment.

116. Remember, my son, that the most valuable thing is to possess nothing.

117. Possessing makes us fools.[98]

---

[95] Cf. 1 Cor 13:7.
[96] Cf. St. Teresa of Jesus, *Interior Castle*, VI, 10,7.
[97] Cf. Mt 18:3.
[98] Cf. Ps 49:12.

118. If you want to, you can be holy. If you decide to be holy, you will be happier, God will help you, he will give you a share of his humility, of his patience, of his love... he will give you a share of himself... his own Spirit.

119. If you have the Spirit of God, there is a column of fire[99] between yourself and heaven that guides men to salvation.

120. If you have the constant remembrance of God and his love, you will become holy.

121. When you awaken, let your first thought be for the Lord.

122. He who prays, fights. To pray is to give blows to the devil. Prayer, even if you don't feel like it, always bears fruit.

123. He who does not pray, sins. He who sins, kills himself. Force yourself to pray. Courage!

124. The terror that you might abandon me and I might fall into Hell... I have nothing, I am nothing, only You... My God!

---

[99] Cf. Ex 13:21; Nb 14:14.

125. Grant me, Lord, the grace not to judge the negligent and not be scandalized by any sinner. *I am negligent, I am a sinner.* Have mercy on me, my God!

126. Grant me to love you, Lord.

127. Your holiness, your glory, your immense love around me.
The air, the light, the rain, my body, my muscles, everything is holy, everything is a creation of love for me. I am in You, I live from You, my life is received, accepted and saved by You. In holiness and justice, in your presence,[100] everything is holy: living, eating, sleeping, thinking, existing. You permeate me, you hold me, you love me, you surround me, you save me, you carry me like a mother carries her little child on her bosom,[101] full of joy and tenderness.
You invite me to live in You a life of holiness in a constant liturgy, worshipping you in my heart, spiritual worship, dwelling within me, grateful, remembering You constantly and telling You, "You are wonderful!" To sing to you, bless you, exult in You, seeing that You do everything well.
My Jesus! My Lord and my God.[102] Who am I?... How is it possible? You, my God, have known contempt, insults, calumny, betrayal, torture, wretchedness, abandonment... the cross. You

---
[100] Cf. Lk 1:75.
[101] Cf. Is 40:11.
[102] Cf. Jn 20:28.

offered yourself on the cross like a little lamb offered on an altar. You allowed yourself to be bound, saying nothing. Poor little lamb: they took You from the flock, brought You to the sacrifice, immolated You in the afternoon, buried You at night…[103] and with You they brought all of humanity to the tomb.

Where are you going so early in the morning? It is cold and the dawn is just beginning to break. Women, where are you going in such a hurry? Come and see where they had laid him, he is not here, he has risen! Go and tell everyone.

To go to Galilee, there they will see him, in Galilee of the gentiles.[104] New Evangelization. He goes before us into Galilee.

He has rescued humanity from the depth of the pit,[105] he has brought us to Heaven. With our eyes fixed on Jesus, Risen and alive, glorious, seated at the right hand of the Father, let us run the race of faith.[106] We will soon die, soon we will be with Him. Without stopping, going toward Him. Our eyes fixed on heaven, where perfect communion, perfect unity, awaits us.

"So that the love with which you have loved me may be in them and I in them…"[107] He has left us love, the Paraclete, the witness, the holy consoler;

---

[103] Cf. Melito of Sardis, *On the Pasch*, 65-67.
[104] Cf. Mt. 28:1-10.
[105] Cf. Ps 86:13.
[106] Cf. Heb 12:2; Ph 3:12.
[107] Cf. Jn 17:26.

in Him he has not left us orphans,[108] in Him we possess immortality. In Him we are infinitely loved, infinitely forgiven, understood. In Him is the holy mercy of God in which we are regenerated, begotten again, forgiven again. Oh! Holy Spirit, thanks to You, I believe in the Father, I believe in the Son, I know everything. I live in the One. I am one with the One. I know that the Father, the Son and the Spirit are one true God in three distinct persons.

128. Where does your not accepting yourself come from? From what concept, from what ideal of happiness or from what projection of yourself? Does your history not seem good to you? What is it that bothers you? What is the cause of your suffering or that concept, that being that oppresses you? From what perspective do you not accept yourself? God loves you as you are, there, where you are; if you don't love yourself, if you don't accept yourself, it's because you are projecting yourself from an *idol*.

We preach Christ and Christ crucified.[109] He is the Lord. To believe in Him, to live in Him, is to accept everything, to live His life... It is to destroy all idolatry.

---

[108] Cf. Jn 14:16-18.
[109] Cf. 1 Cor 1:23; 2:2.

129. *Lord, Jesus, to feel you,*
To feel love for you,
my Jesus, inside,
deep inside,
and to cry from the love and tenderness,
because You are the sweetest thing,
the best,
the holiest.
To love you and love you so much.
You are my God,
You are love,
You are the secret soul of everything,
You are the hidden mystery
because of your humility
and because of your love and tenderness.
To feel you crying inside,
very deep inside my soul.

130. *Flooded by your light,*
full of your holiness,
in a chanted liturgy,
life gathered up in your memory,
in the sweetness of your silent love,
hidden, humble, and meek:
your Spirit.
And men don't love You
and You, full of their lovelessness,
with it, you save us.
And they are killing You
and you are saving us
with death itself.

> *Oh! If only*
> *I could burn, full of your holiness:*
> *fire, fusion of love,*
> *spirit, light:*
> *my love, help me!*

131. With nothing, dispossessed of everything, even of the very "Book" that I have loved so much, without paintings, without writings, without a house, without friends, only You and heaven. Life is a masterpiece. Living, a holy liturgy. The psalms are a marvelous ritual of your love. My poverty and contemplation of You. Your Spirit is very close, close to my heart, like a friend and companion along the way. "Excellent consoler, sweet guest of the soul."[110] Divine prisoner in the tabernacle of my own chest. You here. You, my friend. You, my God and protector.

132. Who can separate me from the love that God has for me? What will be strong enough to make God not love me? Death? Life? The heights? Sin? If I look at Christ crucified for me, who died for me so that I may not die, who loves me to the point of death, who loves me, yes, who loves me so much... Who will separate us from the love of God, made known to us in Christ Jesus?[111]

---

[110] Cf. *Sequence of the Mass of Pentecost.*
[111] Cf. Rom 8:35,39.

133. Mamma! My mother! From my abasement, from my deep reality of sin, I invoke You, holy mercy, total mercy, mercy of God. You love me and protect me so much.

134. The seal that marks us as "Christ's own" is humility.

135. If God grants you the holy humility of Christ, you will be happy.

136. What does it mean to be humble? To prefer Christ's love to everything else.

137. What is being humble? Welcoming contempt and offenses with an inner joy, out of love for Jesus.

138. How I wish my life were a liturgy of holiness, a new worship in which gratitude to You and your love were constant! You are an artist: the trees are sculptures, the light that moves is a wonder, the air, the fields, the birds, the flowers, the storm, the scent of rain, the shadows…, history, time… what a mystery is time: it runs or stops, passes slowly or flies, and it's already gone.

139. We Christians have no other duty than communion. Judging like Martha, who does all the household duties while judging Mary,[112] destroys *koinonia*. To walk without judging. "I desire mercy

---

[112] Cf. Lk 10:38-42.

and not sacrifice," says the Lord.[113] We owe each other love "as I have loved you,"[114] his love when we are sinners.

140. When I look down, my heart freezes. How terrifying, my God!

141. Blessed are You, Lord, holy and immaculate, compassionate, full of sweetness and goodness, merciful, infinitely merciful, thrice holy. Father, our heavenly Father, may your name be kept holy through your holy Church.
Give me *zeal* for your house that it may consume me,[115] may it make of me innocent, a little one, a poor one: You alone in me. May love for your Church, zeal for your house, devour me, may its fire burn up all avarice in me, all possessiveness, may it make me innocent, may it give me *innocence*. There is nothing innocent in me without your Holy Spirit, without the fire of your love that devours me, that makes me love your Church: that fire gives you glory. Your Spirit sears me, gives me zeal for your house, which makes me small, poor, innocent. Purifying the source of my ego, made little, I can offer my life as a liturgy: my acts will be pure. Without innocence, there is no *ritual purity*. All the acts of my history are a liturgy of holiness; the Sacred Scriptures are its ritual. Zeal, innocence,

---

[113] Cf. Mt 9:13; 12:7.
[114] Cf. Jn 13:34.
[115] Cf. Ps 69:9; Jn 2:17.

purity. May ritual purity be accompanied by true temperance, by the *dominion over self*, so that my libations not be made at Aphrodite's table and I not sacrifice on the altar of so many idols. Grant me, O Lord, strength, courage, zeal, love for your Church, innocence, purity of heart, dominion over myself, *holiness*, but above all *humility*. Without your Son's humility of heart, there is nothing. Meekness, humility of heart, eyes fixed on the crucified Jesus. Only the humility of Christ has truly consoled me. How many times I have found consolation and rest in it. Oh, holy humility of Christ! Clothe me in yourself. You are the altar of my holocaust, of my priesthood, of the little liturgy I must officiate at every day.

Your Spirit,
which gives me zeal for your house
that devours me
and burns up the impurity of my intention,
makes me innocent,
little, poor.
Makes my sacrifice of praise
pure,
helps me to be vigilant,
to have dominion over myself,
gives me humility,
holy humility,
where You are
and the peace of your love
and rest can be found.

There is no humility without *fear*, fear of sin, of sinning mortally, of falling into the terrible abyss. Fear, "holy fear," a gift of your Spirit, which leads us to raise our eyes to You, to pray, which brings us to the gift of *piety*, to love you, to desire you, to grow in the *Holy Spirit*, to be clothed in the gift of *prophecy*. Baptism makes us prophets. Zeal, innocence, purity, temperance, humility, fear, piety, prophecy, ardor, love, martyrdom.

Prophetic charism! How necessary you are to the Church. There is no true catechesis that is not also prophecy. To evangelize is to prophesy. To form catechists is to have them walk this itinerary (zeal – innocence – ritual purity – dominion over self – humility – fear-- piety – Spirit – prophecy),[116] it is to help them to be prophets, it is to have them descend the steps of Baptism that makes us kings, prophets and priests. For your greater glory. Amen.

Pieve di Cadore, July 30, 1990.

142. My life is holy because You are in it. My history is holy because You make it, You lead it, You carry it. If you were not present, my life would be dark, cold, without light, full of demands, of slavery. I am a sinner. Your patience with me moves me, it surprises me how holy you are, how patient, how merciful.

143. There is nothing on earth greater than humility.

---

[116] Cf. Mishnah, Sotah, IX:15.

144. What is humility? Christ, our Lord, crucified.

145. What is love? Christ, our Lord, crucified. What is mercy? Christ, our Lord Jesus, crucified.

146. Grant me, Lord, zeal for your house, may it devour me, may it consume all the impurity of my soul, zeal for them to know You and the one you have sent, Jesus Christ.[117] New Evangelization. Love for your Church, for the liturgy. The Church, *semper reformanda*.[118] May zeal for You make me innocent, destroy all avarice in me. *Ad majorem Dei gloriam.* Your glory, Lord. That full of your innocence, of You, my sacrifice may please you, my oblation be pure, my life be a liturgy of holiness, may it be full of ritual purity, may it bring me to self-control, may it make me know who I really am, my weakness, may it give me discernment, make me humble – holy humility of Christ, where the heart rests! – may it give me the humility to begin each day anew, the humility to be patient with myself. May humility bring me to the holy fear of sinning, of falling into the deep abyss, and may that lead me to the need to pray, to the humility that makes me holy, and gives me your Spirit. May your Holy Spirit make me a witness of your Son, may it give me the spirit of prophecy so that I may be a *prophet of your glory*, which is your Word that creates everything, that

---

[117] Cf. Jn 17:3.
[118] Cf. *Gaudium et spes*, 43; *Unitatis redintegratio*, 6.

judges everything. "I see heaven open and a white horse; he who rides it wears a cloak soaked in blood...His name is 'Word of God'... And some thrones were prepared and they took their seats and were given the power to judge".[119]

147. September 6, 1990.
A wonderful letter from the Holy Father to Bishop Cordes,[120] recognizing the good that the Neocatechumenal Way does in the Church. This is the good with which You, Lord Jesus, repay my evil. Always, in return for my sins, infidelities, betrayals, You are good to me. From me, you receive the cross, insults, scourging and death, and from You I receive resurrection, forgiveness, the Holy Spirit, love, affection, tenderness...
Blessed be your holy Name!
"May the peoples praise You,
may all the peoples praise you."[121]
May they celebrate your Name, row upon row.
May they sing joyfully:
How great is the Lord Yahweh Sabaoth!
May the kings of the earth raise their eyes
and contemplate holiness, goodness, love,
all these raised upon a cross,
full of victory in the figure of Christ,

---

[119] Cf. Rev. 19:11,13; 20:4.

[120] Cf. John Paul II, *Epistula R. P.D. Paulo Josepho Cordes, Delegato "in personam" ad Communitates Novi Catechumenatus* (8-30-1990): *AAS* 82 (1990) 1513-1515.

[121] Cf. Ps 67:5.

the Servant who offers himself like a little lamb
for each man on earth.
Grain of wheat fallen into the furrow,
who dies to bear fruit.[122]
He who knows You, he who knows your love,
he who has felt your goodness and your caress,
is marked forever.

148. Convivence in Porto San Giorgio, September 1990. 570 young men aspiring to enter the seminary. 10 new *Redemptoris Mater* seminaries open. Everyone has left happy, and I... am dying. I am left with nothing. Your voice alone sustains me before the traps of the devil. "Courage, Kiko, I will help you!" To accept your love over my nothingness. Make me love you a little, Lord!

149. O Lord, may I cover the multitude of my sins with mercy toward others![123] I am a wretch. I don't deserve to be called your son.[124] Have mercy! The enemy pursues me.[125] I am on the verge of falling. You will help me. I will not waver. By your goodness and glory, by your immense compassion, save me, that I may not be condemned, Lord.

---

[122] Cf. Jn 12:24.
[123] Cf. 1 P 4:8.
[124] Cf. Lk 15:19.
[125] Cf. Ps 143:3.

150. I was hard pressed, but the Lord came to help me.[126] They laid a snare for my steps and I was on the verge of falling, but the Lord came to help me. And in the midst of the anguish and the snare of the net, his powerful voice, "I will help you." And the Lord helped me. The net was broken and I was freed like a bird from the fowler's snare.[127] The devil, furious, will attack again. You will help me. How good you are, Lord! I would like you to be happy with me, and, nonetheless, I feel I am a poor thing, a sinner. I emerge from this fight battered and poor. Finally saved, thanks to You, who worked the miracle. They wanted me to "sacrifice". I was imprisoned and You spoke to me from within, "I will help you!" I felt lost and only your voice, "I will help you!" And the Lord helped me. And I was saved from the pit, from the mortal trap of death. You sustained me. Blessed be you, Lord!

151. I am left with nothing. Without works, naked, ready for judgement and condemnation. "Eat, drink, get drunk, beat the servants."[128] This is how I am. My God! My God! Only your mercy. I live by your grace. I am in your mercy. I only have a little light left that keeps my souls alive: *you don't reject me, you love me*. Yes, you love me![129] Infinitely merciful.

---

[126] Cf. Ps 118:13.
[127] Cf. Ps 124:7.
[128] Cf. Lk 12:45.
[129] Cf. Ps 22:8-9.

Infinitely holy. You, my God, my beloved Jesus. Have mercy on me, Lord, for I am a sinner.

152. I am left with nothing. I have only You. I have no virtue, no prayer, no mortification, nor sacrifice; I have nothing but sin and lustful thoughts, terrors that come and go, sloth, emptiness. You, only You. The Way, art, painting... nothing, only You. Have mercy. Will I be condemned? So many people who do not know You live as prisoners to sins and vices that make them suffer, that rob them of life that is You. And me? I deserve punishment and death. Have mercy! Have mercy! Help me, my Jesus. Help me. Don't leave me, for I will betray You. Don't be distracted even for a moment, for I will be lost. Look, sin besieges me. The devil fences me in, circling round and round.[130] You will help me. I will not waver. The Virgin Mary prays for me from heaven. What a bad son I am. You, Mother of Jesus, help me. Forgive my enemies. Help them.

153. I emerge from one battle and begin another. The enemy doesn't leave me alone for even a moment. Important things must be happening if the devil is so furious... My God! My God! Your voice, your love, your mercy, how good you are to me.
Woe is me, for I am a sinner! Woe is me, for I do not practice what I preach![131] Woe is me, for I will

---

[130] Cf. 1 P 5:8.
[131] Cf. Mt 23:3.

be condemned if I do not convert! Jesus, my Jesus, your name is sweet and...

How many battles, what a mess, how can we go on? The families, the itinerants, the Way, the Bishops, the seminaries... Woe is me! Who will help me? We return from Tokyo and we are poor little things, a tiny boat in the midst of a stormy sea. Virgin Mary, help us! Mother of mine, pray for me. I am a wretch. You work wonders and miracles and I will be condemned. You are with us and I am a sinner, an indecent man, a wicked man, a worthless man, a hypocrite... My God! My God! The martyrs of Tsuwano impressed me. Moscow, Tokyo, Japan, Russia. How many people who do not know You. I see the chalice of your blood raised in the Eucharist and in it the nations converted and saved. Yes, You exist. Yes, You are present. You love us. You will save us.

December 21, 1990

154. Lord Jesus, my love. I am suffering so much. My reality, my total weakness overwhelms me. Only your light weighs on me, your election.

Your call, your election, is my glory. But I? Nothing! Dirt. I am like a dead planet that shines from afar by the light of the sun, a planet that reflects your light, but, if you get closer to it, like the moon, it's dirt, dust, nothing. That's me: nothing, plus sin.[132]

---

[132] Cf. St. Catherine of Siena.

Your election over me is totally gratuitous. Why me? Your love for me... One hundred new families depart to evangelize. Meeting with the Pope. Me, with no voice, exhausted. At my limit. Close to collapsing. One hundred families with many children. They are departing for Russia, China, etc. What do you want from me? The psychological tension is enormous. Who am I? You strip me of everything, and You... I am afraid of going crazy. The nervous tension, physical and moral fatigue, the devil who tempts me, "Kill yourself!" My God! My God, help me! These are signs of stress, of exhaustion. You will help me, I will not succumb, the devil will not succeed. You will win, you will take me with you, we will evangelize this generation, you will take me to heaven. I am a poor fellow... it doesn't matter. The important thing is You, is your love for me, is your holiness, is your glory, is You crucified for me. Full of humility, of meekness.

Little Paschal lamb.

155. I know of You what you have allowed me to know.[133] And what I know is that You are so good: humble, meek, little, full of goodness. That you come to my aid. That You pity me so much. Every time I have cried to you in my anguish, You have helped me and history has turned in my favor. Every morning You renew me with your grace, with

---

[133] Cf. Lk 10:22.

your support, You invite me to begin again. Don't leave me, Lord. Don't leave me.

156. Give me humility; give me strength to do what You ask of me. Courage, strength, which come from You, from your being *Kyrios*, Lord of all, seated at the right hand of God. Humility, strength, courage, bravery, discernment, prudence, fear, holy fear.

I have to act with strength, with the strength of faith, with the strength that God asks of me, to help people, the families, the seminaries… The *catechumenia*, America, Russia, Japan…and my weakness, alone and a sinner. Your love, your total love. Through the Holy Spirit, You give yourself to me totally. In Christ crucified, God was reconciling the world to himself.[134] Christ is God, fully God, image of the divine essence.[135] Given totally for my sins, to the point of death, so that I may receive Him, Him fully, not a part, Him entirely. This is why he gives me his Spirit. The Spirit is God, wholly God. The Father is God, the Son is God, the Holy Spirit is God. One God in three distinct persons. Oh Holy Trinity! Blessed Trinity. "Oh my Three!"[136] My beloved Three in us: humility is perfect, love is perfect, compassion, mercy… my God, my God, the love with which you loved Christ you have deposited in me, it is in me. The love of the Father was in the Son loving me to the point of

---

[134] Cf. 2 Cor 5:19.
[135] Cf. Heb 1:3.
[136] Cf. Bl. Elizabeth of the Trinity.

death and death on a cross.[137] The Father, the Son, the Love, and I in Them.

If God the Father deposits the love that he has for Christ in me, in this love is the Father and the Beloved, the Son, and They Three in me. "May the love with which you have loved me be in them and I in them."[138]

157. Remember, my son, that for your works to be Christian, they must have an eschatological, heavenly meaning, that is: their reward is in heaven.[139] That is why the Lord places a veil to cover your eyes from the good you are doing, so that you do not glorify yourself and lose your heavenly reward. This veil is made of temptations. There has been given to each of us, like to St. Paul, an angel of Satan whose mission is to throw us to the ground, to humiliate us.[140] It has been given to us as a help in the mission so that we do not glorify ourselves and lose our reward.

158. Without humility, there is nothing.

159. Whoever does not accuse himself, accuses the others.

---

[137] Cf. Phil 2:8.
[138] Jn 17:23.
[139] Cf. Mt 6:1,4,6.
[140] Cf. 2 Cor 12:7.

160. Heaven awaits us. Here there is no true rest. Raise your eyes to heaven: happiness lies there.

161. Our job is humility. If you have occasion to bear contempt, injuries or insults, the Lord is offering you the shortest route. It's a proof of his love. Bear them! This surpasses all the virtues… Christ crucified is the radiant light of the love of God.

162. Humility is a path that leads to heaven: sicknesses, old age, the contempt of your relatives or children or your boss or your own wife, your job, etc.; a way that has its reward in heaven. In this way, in this path, the luminous footsteps of Christ precede us.[141] We must follow them, in the constant remembrance of Him, crucified for you, and of his infinite love. Rejoice and little by little get closer to Him, crucified. Sickness, old age and death make us small and holy.

163. He who doubts that God and others love him is arrogant: he will suffer a lot. Never doubt the love that God has for you. To doubt it is not to believe that Christ truly crucified Himself for you, a sinner.

164. Every sin is a lie. The devil is the father of lies.[142] To sin is to be deceived; it's to believe a lie. There

---

[141] Cf. 1 P 2:21.
[142] Cf. Jn 8:44.

is not a single man who has ever sinned and been happy.

165. Lord, make me able to win today, grant me the victory that comes from You. I get up and I say, "Grant Lord, that I can win today."

166. Your grace moves me, Lord. The more despondent I am, you visit me and, graciously, freely, because you want to, you renew me, and you relieve me... How good you are, Lord!

167. Psalm
Your ways, Lord,
your ways.
On the hidden path,
amid the commotion
of crossroads,
of paths and tracks,
of freeways, of bridges,
in Babylon,
a path, a way
full of your footprints.
A footpath of mercies,
like a little river,
a silent way,
in Babylon,
in the midst of Sodom,
leads toward You.
To its right, an abyss:
pride of the heart;

> *to the left, a precipice:*
> *the desires of the flesh,*
> *the passions, the pleasures,*
> *the lusts.*
> *Along your paths,*
> *along your way,*
> *towards You,*
> *following your footprints*
> *like a little river,*
> *my spirit goes and sings*
> *and is moved*
> *and doesn't know what to do*
> *to Love you.*
> *You are today and tomorrow,*
> *I know not.*
> *You are today and tomorrow,*
> *I will wait.*

168. Brasilia, Lima, Medellin, Santo Domingo... You precede us, doing miracles for the *Redemptoris Mater* seminaries. Your presence, your love, your peace. New Evangelization with the Pope, and in Christ everything is possible for us.

169. We are in Paris and the dirty, empty churches make me sad. My heart burns while I walk along the streets and see so many people who have abandoned the Church. How can one help them? By evangelizing.

170. The devil doesn't leave me, he fences me in, he chases me, he insinuates himself, he retreats and charges again, and I, more tired than ever, and I cry to You, "Lord Jesus, my love, save me!"

171. Do you want to have discernment? Renounce everything, remain alone with Him. "Alone with the Only One." One on one, two in one flesh.[143] Despise the world and its vainglory. In how you dress, in where you are, in what you do, only his will, in the liturgy of your life: contempt and mockery, persecution and calumnies upon the altar of Christ, which is his cross. Remember that it has to be accepted in freedom, chosen by you out of love, by grace.
In this liturgy, You want my life to be your Word: "Christ." Obeying your Word, Christ. May my actions put your Word into practice, your Word: "Christ." You want my words to You to be the ineffable groaning of your Spirit, that from always has groaned[144] toward You: breath, prayer, recognizing always my sins that have crucified your Son. Toward men, speaking of You, giving them your Word: "Christ." May my thoughts be your love toward me, your Word: "Christ." My life, Christ crucified. My actions, Christ crucified.[145] My word, Christ crucified. My thoughts, Christ

---

[143] Cf. Eph 5:31.
[144] Cf. Rom 8:26.
[145] Cf. Gal 2:20.

crucified for me. My love: for You, my God, holy and humble, full of compassion and mercy toward me, I who do everything full of negligence, sloth, who do everything badly. Full of temptation, always groaning toward You.
To love you, Lord, is my only happiness, and to love your Church. And to see Christ in every man, accepting that so many times I can do nothing. Not to possess anything, not even my own will, nothing, only Him and His wisdom. Does communion with Carmen and Mario mean to die to my own will at every moment? "Alone to alone." In Him, everyone.

172. Whoever does not accept to live day by day is arrogant and ambitious; he doesn't seek God, he seeks himself, his plans, his idols.

173. I am in… Yesterday we had a meeting with the priests of the diocese and the Cardinal was present … More than 100 priests attended. It was raining cats and dogs. A difficult atmosphere. They wouldn't let Carmen speak. Attacks... The Lord helped us.
I am a wretch. Last night I watched television for a while. Today a lightning bolt struck the antenna and destroyed it… A sign of your love for me and your disgust with my negligence. Lord, You take me out of a thousand traps by working constant miracles. How good you are. You do it to help me in the mission. How many graces I will have to account for… The rain keeps pouring.

174. I am painting the apse of the parish of St. Frances Cabrini in Rome. It's enormous, almost 100 square meters. On top of that, it's slanted and has several pleats that make everything more difficult. To paint is to preach the Gospel. One paints with the soul. Help me, Lord! I am without Carmen or Mario, in the midst of a terrible battle: the problems with the wall, temptations, the devil, the Way, the seminaries, the families in mission, the enemies who hate us, the devil's subtle but terrible traps… You save me; you help me. How good you are, Lord! Holy, holy, holy is the Lord, God of hosts! Heaven and earth are full of your glory. Hosanna! Hosanna! Blessed is he who comes.

    I'm going to be condemned; I'm a wretch who endangers the immense gifts God has given me to help the Church. I, unworthy and evil, despising everything, and, for love of my passions, I approach sin and oblige the Lord to do miracles to take me out of dangerous situations… *I am a total impediment,* a useless servant.[146] How patient you are with me. Have mercy, Lord, have mercy! The enemy stalks me, haunts me. Virgin Mary, help me, my mother, save me, love me, pray for me.

175. Help me today, that I may win. Help me to convert. You, only You. My soul full of You, full of light. One paints with the soul. One paints with You inside.

---

[146] Cf. Lk 17:10.

176. Look, Lord, that on my way they have laid a snare for me.[147] They have laid a trap and I'm at the point of falling. You, Lord, help me! You are my portion on this earth, "My only happiness."[148] The saints will rejoice with me because You came to my help; You saved me. I see myself as lost… Don't take away my trust that You will help me.

177. My son, do not descend from the cross, because you will suffer a lot. Take up your cross and follow me.[149] I will take you to heaven.

178. "Where have You hidden, beloved, and left me moaning… Ay, who will be able to heal me…"[150] Look, the pain of love is not cured but with the presence and the figure… Have mercy on me, Lord. Have mercy! I am a sinner, a wretch, a traitor, a wicked man, an ignoble being… What can you love in me who am such a great sinner? To kill oneself or believe that You love me…? You sustain the depth of my being, by grace. Have patience with me. My debt is great.[151]

If You exist,
if you truly love me so much,
only dying is important.

---

[147] Cf. Ps 142:4.
[148] Cf. Ps 142:5.
[149] Cf. Mt 16:24.
[150] St. John of the Cross, *Spiritual Canticle*.
[151] Cf. Mt 18:26.

To be with You.
United to You,
in total humility.
And the world will be transformed.

179. If you descend from the cross, the devil will devour your very depths.

180. And on the cross, to say with you, "Father, forgive them, for they know not what they do."[152] And when everything becomes difficult, to say along with the good thief, "Remember me, Lord, now that you are in your Kingdom, " in order to hear in the depth of the heart, "This day you shall be with me in Paradise."[153] In this liturgy of holiness, which is to be on the cross with our Lord Jesus, feeling him telling you, "Behold your *Mother*."[154] Yes, she helps me not to descend from the will of God, not to sin. She has known in her heart the pain of sin in the flesh of her Son, she knows, she understands, she will help you. She, who is alive in heaven, prays for me. "*Eli, Eli, lama sabactani.*"[155] Everything is written. Psalm 22 is a ritual of holiness. The *Psalter* is the ritual of a new and heavenly liturgy, which culminates shouting to the Lord, "Father, into your hands, I commend my spirit!"[156] To go with you, to

---
[152] Lk 23:34.
[153] Cf. Lk 23:42-43.
[154] Jn 19:27.
[155] Cf. Ps 22:1; Mt 27:46.
[156] Lk 23:46.

be with you. On the cross, on an altar, fulfilling the *Shema*, loving You, Lord, my God, with all my heart, with all my mind, with all my strength, in the total surrender to our neighbor.[157]

181. Lord Jesus, my dearest God, the enemy pursues me, temptation shakes me like a gale... May the roots of my faith, firm in your love, help me resist and not fall.

182. I am negligent man, a sinner. You have given me your Holy Spirit in Baptism so that I may bury in it my passions and sins. You have reawakened me, like Lazarus,[158] for my conversion. Your Spirit guides me, and I mistreat it. He speaks to me of You, and I want to satisfy myself with the husks of swine.[159] Your infinite mercy and your patience toward me move me. They do well to persecute me. I am a wretch, ungrateful and, if I continue like this, you will have to take away my "talent."[160] I am negligent, a sinner, wicked, a traitor... I only deserve contempt. You have awakened me like Lazarus not to condemn me... Have mercy!

183. The love that the Father has for the Son is so great, so great that they are perfectly One. The Father is in the Son *as one*, and the Son is in the Father *as one*,

---

[157] Cf. Dt 6:4-5; Mk 12:30.
[158] Cf. Lk 11:43.
[159] Cf. Lk 15:16.
[160] Cf. Mt 25:28.

and this is fulfilled in the Spirit. "May the love with which You have loved me be in them and I in them. So that they may be perfectly one and the world may believe. I in them and You in Me."[161]

In this perfect unity is the whole mystery of the Church: her essence, her nature, her mission.

184. "Lord, set a sentinel at my mouth, a guard at the door of my lips. May the just man strike me out of love and correct me, so that my heart may not incline to evil, to commit criminal acts…"[162] I am that man, a hypocrite, wicked. Woe is me! Unhappy me, I have the reputation of a saint and yet I do evil. Miserable. Have pity on me, Lord. Have pity, have patience, I will repay you everything.[163] Have patience with me. You have chosen the wrong man. I came out wrong. Did you put your trust in a fool…? My Jesus! My Jesus! My sins are innumerable, enormous and great, but your mercy is infinite, immense, absolute. I have offended you, have pity. I have fallen into the traps of the devil. You save me with your cross. You are the only one in whom I believe. Holy little Virgin, Mother of Jesus and my Mother, I do not deserve to be your son.

Today is the feast of the Assumption: August 15, 1992. *Receive my prayer.*

---

[161] Cf. Jn 17:21-23.
[162] Cf. Ps 141:3-5.
[163] Cf. Mt 18:26.

*May it be my conversion
as an offering before You,
as a gift for your feast.
May I be a paladin
of your love,
of your mercy
for the sinner.
I look to heaven,
and the mist of your mercy
consoles my heart
burned by sin.
How horrible the hell of passion,
the implacable demons
who hurl into nothingness.
I look at the earth,
and hardness everywhere,
demonic law
of legalisms without forgiveness.
Christ crucified
for the sinners,
for me,
and my Mother below,
offered with Him
for the salvation of the fallen ones
in the infinite traps,
in the endless nets of the malevolent,
of so many enemies.
Forgive me, Lord.
and with you I will begin again.
I will live as a paroled prisoner.
Give me humility of heart.*

185. Five new *Redemptoris Mater* seminaries are born: Kaohsiung, Perth, Vienna, Lugano, and Guadalajara (Mexico). 700 young men willing to go anywhere. And I? A demon was eating up my soul, bite by bite. Hell before me, fire inside, the fire of the flames of no love. Only your voice, "Courage, Kiko, I am with you."[164] The devil, infuriated by so many young men, so many vocations, the seminaries, wants to devour me. Help me, Lord. Have pity, my Jesus!

186. Every person has the right to possess God in hope.

187. I am a sinner, a wicked man who puts the marvelous work that God is doing in danger, for his own pleasure. Lord! Lord! Come! Holy Spirit who loves the sinner, who is attracted to those who confess that they are ill and sinners, come, Spirit of goodness, of mercy, of sweetness, of meekness, of understanding, of profound tenderness, of infinite affection... Holy Spirit, come and help me... Do not rebuke me in your anger, do not reprove me in your wrath,[165] have patience, Lord; I will repay you everything.[166] Give me another opportunity; I am a wretch. The Holy Father has inaugurated the *Redemptoris Mater* seminary of Santo Domingo. 13 cardinals and 60 bishops came. It was extremely

---

[164] Cf. Is 43:1-2,5; Ac 18:9-10.
[165] Cf. Ps 6:1.
[166] Cf. Mt 18:26.

hot. Lord, how great You are. Have mercy, the enemy knocks me down, help me!

188. My son, have patience with yourself. Get up; begin again. Courage, *I love you more and more!* We already know you are a sinner, unworthy, a traitor and a wretch, but… be patient: it is the sick who need a doctor.[167] Courage; I love you; I forgive you; I love and save you! Be patient with your reality and begin again. Courage, I love you more and more.

189. November 1992.
I am in Denver (Colorado). We have been travelling for nearly a month: Santo Domingo, Ecuador, Chile, Brazil, Guatemala, Venezuela, El Salvador, Mexico, and now, Denver, Washington, New York, Paris, etc. We have visited the families in the most poor and miserable areas of America, full of sects. Their children consoled us, the communities they have formed. People are returning from the sects to the Church.
At my side, a devil humiliates me,[168] he won't leave me. So I have to raise my eyes constantly toward You, my God, my love, my consolation.
We have spoken in Mexico to the Episcopal Conference. I think it went very well. So many congratulated us. I always see in the bishops the fullness of the sacrament of Holy Orders. They

---

[167] Cf. Mt 9:12.
[168] Cf. 2 Cor 12:7.

make me feel tenderness and love for your Church. In each country we had a meeting with the priests who follow the Way. I encouraged them to keep doing it. "Lust, fornication, pornography destroy the roots of faith, they make them decay little by little, turning you into a cynic." This I told them, inviting them to get back up, to come out of such suffering. It was wonderful. Two of them came to speak with me recognizing that they found themselves in that situation. I told them to ask the bishop for permission to go itinerant, abandoning that situation of entrapment, suffering, and betrayal.

To love the priests, to help them, to give them a community to walk in. We have seen that a Beast is coming out of the abyss to fight against the Lamb.[169] It has three heads: nationalism, exacerbated enculturation, and ecology raised to the point of nature worship. These three heads feed each other and rise up against the Evangelization. Your love sustains my roots.

190. That you may be justified when you give sentence and be without reproach when you judge.[170] How holy You are, and I such a scoundrel! I have sinned, Lord. I am a wretch. But... have patience, I will repay You everything.[171] Stop the Angel who comes

---

[169] Cf. Rev. 17:13-14.
[170] Ps 51:4.
[171] Cf. Mt 18:26.

to punish me; wait a moment. I am afraid, Lord. You know how to free the righteous from their trials and keep the impious for punishment on the day of judgement.[172] I am that impious man who doesn't deserve anything other than to be trampled underfoot like salt that has lost its flavor.[173] Please, Lord, have pity on me. Come to my help. The enemy, full of furor, tramples my life into the ground.[174] Have pity. The more you enlighten me to speak and preach, the weaker I become, more sinful, more suffering, more the feeling that if I continue like this, I will be condemned. May the desire to evangelize that You place in my heart, the fire of your love, burn the impurities that the enemy sows in my spirit. Amen.

191. Whoever does not possess the glory of humility, seeks the glory of men.

192. I give you thanks, Lord, because you have consoled me in the midst of so many sins and afflictions. Your Spirit guides me to pray in the certainty that You love me and that you want me to give you a little space. Though I consider myself the most unfaithful and vile sinner, I know that You love the sinner, that it is your nature to love, love totally, giving all of yourself to the point of death, and this for me, a sinner and traitor. You love me, and this

---

[172] Cf. 2 P 2:9.
[173] Cf. Mt 5:13.
[174] Cf. Ps 7:5.

consoles me in the midst of everything. How holy and good you are! How is it possible for You to continue to love me? I would like to be holy, and you see...

193. The path of the Christian is humility.

194. The crown of the Christian is humility.

195. The land where God accepts sacrifice is humility.[175]

196. The job of a Christian is discernment.

197. Place a sentinel at your heart, and with every thought that tries to enter, ask, "Are you from God or from the enemy?" It will answer.[176]

198. If you wish to have discernment, scorn everything for Him.

199. Hate your wife; hate your children; hate your father and your mother; hate your own life[177] and you will have discernment: alone to alone, and in Him everything.

200. The Christian's mirror: prayer.

---

[175] Cf. *Sayings of the Desert Fathers*.
[176] Cf. ibid.
[177] Cf. Lk 14:26.

201. The Christian's battle: prayer.

202. The Christian's weapon: prayer.

203. The Christian's shield: prayer.

204. To deny oneself, climb up on the cross,[178] and consider the others better than oneself[179] is to have an adult faith.

205. Remember, son, that to whom much is given, much will be asked.[180]

206. Obey Christ, who told you, "Behold your mother,"[181] and bring her with you always, receive her into your house, like St. John.[182]

207. Correction... and my spirit stiffens. And I walk about like a drunkard, tipsy and off-balance... Without You, hell. And it was you who were correcting me. Have pity! Have pity!

208. Nothing is mine. Only You are profoundly mine.

209. If I lack your Spirit, everything is foreign to me: the world, things, and people. The loneliness of the

---

[178] Cf. Mk 8:34.
[179] Cf. Ph 2:3.
[180] Cf. Lk 12:48.
[181] Jn 19:27.
[182] Cf. Jn 19:27.

terrible Hell... Yes, I can love nothing. Yes, I can possess nothing. My soul dead in a matter-less cosmos... the horror of your absence, of evil, without love, in a cold darkness, without matter. Without You, there is no matter.

210. *Only You,*
Lord, my God,
and things continue on, impassively.
Your infinite mercy,
your great compassion,
your love toward me,
freely given.
And I ask myself:
Why do you love me so much?
Who am I,
who betray you,
full of neglect?
Your love wins me over,
possesses me,
makes me one in You.
Your love
and to contemplate my nothingness,
my sinfulness,
and your love.
To remain in You.
To accept You as You are,
my God,
without wanting to change you.
You love me so, so much.
Your love will triumph

*over my pride
of wanting to be...
Your love and that's enough.
And to cry for my sins,
accepting your love
that makes me
suffer for my betrayal.
I behave badly
and You love me,
my Jesus crucified.
Let me weep
upon your breast.*

211. We are in Africa, and in a tent, yesterday, in the midst of this beautiful nature, black men were singing while waving their arms with branches and flowers to receive us. We announced Christ, and they listened, surprised, applauding my words,
"Believe the Good News today, now! Convert and believe so that you may now receive the promised Spirit[183] *now*, the Holy Spirit, who, living within you, allows you to forgive, to love in a new way. Look at this cross: He died for you, he has made a testament to the Father, on your behalf, of his immortal life itself, his Spirit. Believe it now.
While I speak to you, Jesus himself is before the Father, presenting his glorious wounds for you.

---

[183] Cf. Ac 2:38-39.

I am Gabriel, today. You are Mary. Say with her, "May it be done unto me according to Your Word."[184]

Faith comes from hearing.[185] Listen! God loves you and wants to free you from slavery to sin, from the suffering that comes from demanding love, from selfishness, from the terrible slavery to always be seeking your own pleasure, from pride, from lust, from gambling, from drink, from hate, from rivalries, from envy... all things that make you suffer.

The Spirit of the Lord accompanies us, it doesn't let our word fall to the ground, unfulfilled; the Lord fulfills what we say. He is the *Kyrios* lifted up above all principalities, above every ruling force and sovereignty.[186] He is the Lord who will return in glory with the saints to judge the living and the dead.[187] He, who has died for all men, in order to fulfill all justice in his body, offering himself for sin,[188] as a sweet smelling victim, so that in Him, in his body, offered and accepted, conversion is preached for the forgiveness of sins.[189] Christ is risen, the guarantee of our liberation, of the forgiveness of sins. Humanity has been forgiven in Christ. It's possible to receive the Spirit that makes

---

[184] Cf. Lk 1:38.
[185] Cf. Rom 10:17.
[186] Cf. Eph 1:21.
[187] Cf. 2 Tim 4:1; 1 P 4:5.
[188] Cf. Eph 5:2.
[189] Cf. Lk 24:46.

of us a new creation.[190] Being made like Him by the Spirit, children of God, he has shared with us his nature.[191] Victory for all the poor ones! Convert and believe the Good News! Be baptized and you will receive the Holy Spirit.[192] For free!

Fruit of his blood, of his passion, not of our works, so that to Him be the glory."

Africa! God loves you. He welcomes its poor ones who sing to the Holy Spirit… It was wonderful how they listened and, afterward, how they prayed. We are in Kenya. We traveled from Cameroon and before that we were in the Ivory Coast. There, in the Basilica of Yamoussoukro, we had a meeting with 2,000 brothers and sisters. Four bishops and the nuncio were there. It was wonderful. After announcing Jesus Christ, we called for vocations and 40 young people stood up. Now we are departing for Zambia.

Africa! Here, in Kenya, the most important thing in 19 years of preaching has been the total failure. Always rejected. The missionaries don't like us; they see us as "rivals." The changing of priests has been killing the communities little by little. Today, after 19 years, there are barely 7 communities in Kenya. But soon everything will change. To fail is to imitate Christ. To fail is to triumph!

---

[190] Cf. 2 Cor 5:17.
[191] Cf. 2 P 1:4.
[192] Cf. Ac 2:38.

212. To persevere in failure is to give one's life. To give one's life is to announce the Gospel.

213. The ancient Fathers say: the war the soul doesn't want to wage won't last long.[193]

214. Above my weakness, above my ingratitude and my infidelity, your holiness. To know your love, your immense compassion, your infinite mercy... your holiness, to know your holiness that overwhelms me, which surpasses me, which infuses me with terror. My Jesus! My Jesus! Have mercy. Hell devours me.
We finished the convivence of Bishops in Vienna. You have done everything. I, a useless servant,[194] or rather, a total impediment. The devil, furious, prepares traps for me, haunts me, surrounds me,[195] doesn't leave me alone. Your holiness saves me. To evangelize Europe, to bring your Word to men, which opens them to grace, to the power of the Holy Spirit.
Awake, Europe! Listen: Christ has washed you in his blood.[196] Christ has given you his life: take it and live. Live forever! It's free. Live, little one, whipped by the winds, slave of merchants, raped by soldiers. Live! Listen and live forever!
Vienna, April 19, 1993.

---

[193] Cf. *Sayings of the Desert Fathers.*
[194] Cf. Lk 17:10.
[195] Cf. 1 P 5:8.
[196] Cf. Rev. 1:5.

215. One of the clearest signs that the love of God dwells in us is that in whatever we do, we do not seek our own interest.[197]

216. How sad it is to have no one to obey.

217. Only obedience is love. Whoever does not obey, does not love.

218. To obey is to love someone. How sad it is to have no one to obey.

219. Sin, dwelling in us, makes us unable to obey[198] and demands from us and enslaves us to the constant desire to seek pleasure, obliges us to offer ourselves everything, makes us unable to give ourselves to others, makes us unable to love, makes us deeply wretched.

    In our dissatisfaction, we realize that our life has no value, because our acts are selfish. We resign ourselves to being this way and, little by little, we destroy our lives. But Christ died to free us from the slavery to sin, so that we might be free.[199] If we accept the preaching of his love, He sends us his Spirit from heaven that invades us and leads us to donate ourselves, to obey God and man, to love them. Blessed be the Lord, who freed us from the devil and his power! To Him be the glory. Amen.

---

[197] Cf. 1 Cor 13:5.
[198] Cf. Rom 7:17,23.
[199] Cf. Heb 2:14-15.

220. The Spirit comes to us through faith, and faith from preaching.[200] The sacraments seal, nourish, and give faith.

221. Preaching, to be listened to, must be done by someone credible, that is, by someone who gives his life for what he says and who shows by facts that God accompanies him, that He sends the Spirit, because true conversions take place.

222. Never feel sorry for yourself, saying, "How much I suffer." Be humble and say, instead, "How good is the Lord with me, because though I deserve so many punishments for my sins, He sees to it that I lack nothing." Do not listen to the devil who flatters you; listen to the one who corrects and rebukes you.

223. Escape is futile: wherever I go, temptation presents itself. Thanks to this, I must constantly turn to You. If you fall, get up. Fight! Pray. Humble yourself! Fight. You will become wise and will be able to better help others.

224. Lord, You have given us faith and the gift of knowledge to overcome unbelief, the gift of wisdom to discern the attacks of the devil, the subtlety of his traps and deceit, and to renounce him by detesting him.

---

[200] Cf. Rom 10:17.

225. Have pity on me, Lord! Woe is me, Lord! Woe is me! Save me, Lord! Save me! The enemy fences me in, he defeats me. Woe is me! Come to my aid! Temptations, fatigue, illnesses, old age, and death are before me. All these make a person little and holy.

226. I am painting in the church of San Bartholomew in Tuto, in Florence. Each painting is a 'labor', a suffering. I do it for You, for your greater glory. Help me, Lord! Without You, nothing. Nothing!

227. Florence, December 1993
Psalm
May the peoples bless You, Lord,
may all the nations acclaim You,
may they sing for You, our God,
may they exult in your love, Lord,
for your tenderness and compassion,
for your infinite goodness and mercy.
In Him, in Christ,
You descended from the heavens.
You descended by the cosmic ladder
and we saw your face,
full of blood,
tortured and broken.
Without judging us,
You gave all of yourself
until death
and you saved us.

228. How good you are, Lord, how good. We have had the convivence for the itinerant catechists of the whole world. We have chosen 72 as a symbol of the universal mission with which the Lord has entrusts us. The audience with the Pope, his words... wonderful! I think that they are the *Magna Carta* of the Way. We will go out to the byways, go out in the streets, we will shout your name, Lord, and spill our blood. For your greater glory!

229. We finished the convivence of bishops of Africa. The Lord was great! More than 100 bishops and 4 cardinals came. Only a third of them knew the Way. Africa is the future of the Church, the Pope told me personally in the audience, while we were taking a picture at the end. He took me by the hand, telling me, "The future of the Church is Africa." Faith conquers the world.[201] To welcome the Gospel... Lord, help me! May I not be condemned, Lord.

230. Lent 1994.
We are in Paris. I preached in the church of St. Gervais. It was very cold and very dark. The brothers listened for more than three hours. The monks of St. Gervais as well. I raised the cross of Christ, and I called them to convert, to leave sin, because the Lord forgives us and loves us.
To love the sinner is the marvel, the Good News. Christ loves you! He wants to be totally one with

---

[201] Cf. 1 Jn 5:4-5.

you, as he is in the Father.[202] To love a sinner, an imposter, a hypocrite, a liar, a depraved person, a thief, a lustful man, a greedy man, a murderer... to the point of giving one's life for him, that is the Good News. Christ has died for sinners! Christ has died on a cross for you! He has paid your debt. God, his Father, resurrected him as a proof and guarantee of forgiveness. Furthermore, he bequeathed his own life, his Spirit, to you. "Father, may the love with which you have loved Me be in them,"[203] thus Jesus prays at the Last Supper. The Holy Spirit in us. God, the Father, is the love that the Son, Christ, shows us on the cross: love for us, sinners.

The Son is the image of the Father: "imprint of his essence," says the Letter to the Hebrews.[204] This essence is the divine nature, Love, *Caritas* that cannot be separated from us, sinners. He forgives us, cleans us, resurrects us, makes of us a new creation and gives us his Spirit who makes us "children of God,"[205] saints.

Look at the Church! Look how they love one another. The Church is the work of the Father in the Son through the Holy Spirit. This work is born from the side of Christ as a spouse, as a new Eve.

---

[202] Cf. Jn 17:21.
[203] Jn 17:26.
[204] Cf. Heb 1:3.
[205] Cf. Rom 8:14.16.

231. To love: this I have learned. To love, that is, to give oneself, climb upon the cross, to love, without demanding, without judging, without presenting a bill, without wanting the other to change… To love, to donate oneself, to climb up on the cross. To be able to love, to be able to give oneself, to be able to ascend the cross, is the work of Christ: he gave his life for this. He sends us his Spirit who invites us to enter God's constant action, enter into his works. God is love.[206] God gives Himself. God climbs up on the cross. Dead to my ego by my Baptism and alive for God, I receive his Spirit who makes me a child of God.[207] I have been adopted as a child.[208] I share in the essence of God, in his nature.[209] In it I live, move,[210] breathe and sing… And my poor heart? To be able to love is the greatest gift – it is to know You, it is to be saved, it is to be one in You with everyone.

The Father is one in Christ with everyone to the point of death. He has given himself completely, completely given over. The mystery of his Passover, the mystery of his cross, is there, in the Eucharist, in the tabernacle. And how do we live this Spirit that makes us love like Christ, give ourselves like Christ, climb up on the cross with Christ? Through faith. And faith comes, grows and increases

---

[206] Cf. 1 Jn 4:8,16.
[207] Cf. Rom 8:14.
[208] Cf. Eph 1:5; Rom 8:15.
[209] Cf. 2 P 1:4.
[210] Cf. Ac 17:28.

through preaching.[211] And where is preaching done? Where are the messengers, the witnesses who give their life without purse or haversack,[212] the bearers of faith, the heralds, the little children[213] who arouse faith and make it resonate?

232. Have mercy on me, Lord, for I am struggling within myself with these mixed emotions! My soul suffers the heavy load: my weakness, the world against You, and the devil's traps. Have mercy on me, Lord! I am weary and I can barely go on in this battle… Protect me, Lord. Have mercy!

233. *Certain are the woes*
pitiful and complaining,
the rotting souls
of so many lost youths,
who await You,
who will fall in love with You
– You, their friend –
and jubilant, they will shout,
and will give You their lives,
because You have broken their chains,
You have paid their debts.
You opened wide the doors to them,
and You called them to go everywhere,
You invited them to climb up on the cross,
to defy their powerful enemies;

---

[211] Cf. Rom 10:17.
[212] Cf. Mt 10:10.
[213] Cf. Mt 25:40,45.

> *You gave them your forged sword,*
> *You dressed them in your own armor,*
> *and You kissed their lips,*
> *full of love,*
> *while You sent them*
> *to travel the earth.*
> *You with them,*
> *enamored spouse*
> *of so many young women*
> *of so many other young men,*
> *of men and women*
> *who have gone*
> *to give their lives like You.*

234. The Church is the flesh of Jesus. The proud person will always reject the *kenosis* of God. He does not accept the incarnation. There are so many people to whom life itself, sin, and people, lead them to travel a path of *kenosis*, of descent, until they arrive at the cross. There a thief recognizes God in Jesus crucified.[214] "The prostitutes will precede you."[215] Although sin, stealing and being in jail don't always make you humble: the other thief, indeed, insulted the Lord...[216]

The proud person never loves the Church, seeing in her only useless ceremonies, hypocrisy, scandals, laws... It's the faith that God gives to the children,

---

[214] Cf. Lk 23:40-42.
[215] Cf. Mt 21:31.
[216] Cf. Lk 23:39.

to those who become like children,[217] that allows us to see in the Church the body of the Lord.[218] God passes through the sacraments, simple signs, he passes through poor men, sometimes full of sins, who generally do not measure up to the Word they announce. To love the Church is to love your flesh, Lord. "And the two shall become one flesh."[219]

235. I have known the Lord's love, his tenderness toward sinners. His total love is warm, hot, all embracing, it's like a fire that invades the other, wishing to consume him by transforming him. I have felt it working in me toward others and now I ask for it for myself, a sinner. Come, Lord Jesus! Fill me with your warmth, embrace me gently in Yourself, so that I may be one in the anchor of your heart and *I may be consummated in your will.* Your love purifies my sins. The warm wind. The gentle breeze.[220] The breath of your love. The sweet tears. You. Forgive me, Lord!

236. The elderly complain and complain, so that we won't leave them alone. And they tell us, without saying it, to love them, that they are dying and going... into the night. Like children in the end, like children at last.

---

[217] Cf. Mt 18:4.
[218] Cf. Eph 1:22-23.
[219] Cf. Eph 5:31.
[220] Cf. 1 K 19:12.

237. The whole mystery of the Church is found in the fact that God loves me, a sinner. My weak, little, unfaithful, lying, sinful being, and You who come with me without being scandalized, who walk with me without judging me, being my true friend.
The proud person, if he approaches me and sees my weakness and poverty, is scandalized. He can't stand the love of Christ for me, a sinner; he wants the love of Christ to transform me into a superman. Power, strength, money, success... no weakness, failure, sin... The incarnation of God, his *kenosis*, his love for us. And I will go down to Hell. There, in the sewers, among rats and demons, how many people. The lack of mercy is demonic.
The law smashing the one who sinned. They looked triumphantly at Christ on the cross. The proud ones drooled despising the one who fell.
To love sinners. Our civilization crumbles if it strays from this point, summarized thus: Christ, and Christ crucified.[221]
God, in Christ crucified, reconciling men to himself.[222]
The family is destroyed if the one who sins cannot be loved.
The world does not want to forgive. It doesn't know how to forgive, doesn't understand why one ought to forgive.

---

[221] Cf. 1 Cor 2:2.
[222] Cf. 2 Cor 5:19.

The world defends its own: money; the rest doesn't matter. The person who is of the world wants that: money, and searches for it in everything. Money... Money is the projection of oneself, of one's ego; in it one sees triumph, self-realization, to be admired, success...

"Choose today whom you wish to serve... You cannot serve two masters. You cannot serve God and money... Choose!"[223]

The world fools you with its "ways," making you believe that you shouldn't bear anything, no one's sin, that this is the true virtue. The world preaches the opposite of Christ crucified, who took upon himself violence, hatred, evil and sin. The world says: No! You should sue. The woman should denounce her violent or drunk husband, etc. You shouldn't put up with anything. You should separate, divorce... The world hates Christ, because in society "the prince of this world"[224] – the devil – rules. His power is overcome only by preaching Christ crucified.

"Popular missions." More than 1,000 pastors from all over Italy have asked us to do popular missions. A real surprise. We did forty this year in Rome and it was a success. About 30 communities were born as fruit of this.

There was preaching in the streets, on the buses, in the homes, in the stores, in offices, in the banks, in

---

[223] Cf. Jos 24:15; Mt 6:24.
[224] Cf. Jn 12:31; 14:30; 16:11; Eph 2:2.

bars and discos. Everywhere. Processions with the Virgin... Fantastic! We will raise the cross. We will preach Christ. They will persecute us, and we will save the world.

The Church, bride of Christ, full of weaknesses and sins, but holy by the immense love of God. The Church, sacrament of the love that Christ has for all men. Christ, the Bridegroom; the Church, his Bride. Two in one flesh.[225] The Christians in the Church, forgiving each other constantly, accepting the weakness of our neighbor, we manifest the mystery of the love of God. We are all sinners; we are all poor ones. I am the worst: a scoundrel, unfaithful, a liar. Woe is me! Woe is me! Lord, have pity...

Ireland 1994.

238. Blessed are You, Lord, who in your "Only One" have shown your love for me. You have shown your essence, "the imprint of your substance."[226] You are LOVE for me. One in me, totally one in me, who am a sinner, a traitor, a *total impediment*. You love me so much, my Lord, that You have given me the flesh and blood of your Son. What more could you have given me? Grant, Lord, that this flesh and this blood may not be useless in me, that I may not despise your Son's passion. You, my Father, give yourself totally to me and for that you

---

[225] Cf. Eph 5:31.
[226] Cf. Heb 1:3.

give me the grace of your Holy Spirit, Spirit thanks to which I may love as You love mankind. I can feel myself in them, completely given to them. "One," one in everyone. Your mercy, your love for sinners. Your Spirit in me would be a fire that burns my heart. To carry your love. To give them your love to eat, your love to drink. To warm their heart with your love. To give them Yourself through the announcement of the Gospel. Fire that transforms fire. Light from light.[227] Radiant brightness that blinds with its light. Light in light. Incessant glow. Spark that expands in heartbeats of love for so many who are groaning without knowing it… You in them and I in You: one.[228] In the One, all. In You I am in all. In You, light. Holy Mother, forgive me. Pray for me.

Ireland, 1994.

239. To receive insults and love the enemy.[229] Not to judge is to begin to be humble. The judge judges. The one who judges is he who thinks he knows the truth and that it is his… "Do not judge."[230] To receive insults… To love the enemy. To feel the heart enflamed with the fire that all may know the Holy Spirit, that they may receive the love of God. Blood and flesh of Jesus, food of Eternal Life. Death is dead. Victory. Victory. And little Mary

---

[227] Cf. Nicene Creed.
[228] Cf. Jn 17:23.
[229] Cf. Mt 5:11,44.
[230] Cf. Mt 7:1.

beneath the cross, with a sword in her soul,[231] receives the blood of her Son and the water from his side, to be the humblest mother of a new humanity. All the poor children of Mary, the Holy Virgin.

240. The Holy Scriptures, the Bible, the Holy Word of God, is the weapon given us so we remain vigilant, just as a sentinel doesn't keep watch without a weapon to defend his post. When the shadows surround you, draw your weapon, take out your sword, the silver Bible from its leather holster, and read, read… and the shadows retreat, thousands of demons retreat. In the name of the Lord I will defeat them.[232] Sentry!… On guard!

Ireland, 1994.

241. Lord, I want to do your will… Love for the neighbor is your will. "The other is Christ."[233] Give me the grace of your Spirit to love the other as You love him, to the point of giving my flesh and blood. Your Spirit alone propels me and helps me to climb up on the cross. A thousand demons want to devour me. I will humble myself, and I will defeat them.

---

[231] Cf. Lk 2:35.
[232] Cf. Ps 118:10.
[233] Cf. Foundational Marian inspiration of the Neocatechumenal Way: "It is necessary to make Christian communities like the Holy Family of Nazareth, who live in humility, simplicity, and praise: the other is Christ."

Woe is me, for I will be condemned! I am proud, lustful, lazy, vain... Woe is me, for I betray You! Woe is me, for I put at risk everything You do... Two ways: either give my life to my neighbor or give him death by my sins... A thousand demons surround me: in the name of the Lord, I will defeat them.[234] In your name I will humble myself, by your name I shall win and be able to be left with nothing, only with You.

242. Today, Our Lady of Mount Carmel, July 16, 1994. My sins are so many... Holy Mother of Jesus, intercede for me. I pray for Ireland, for her Catholic Church, for the Way. Help me Holy Virgin Mary, Mother of Carmel, Lady of all the prophets. Help the Carmelites. And, above all, help Carmen. Pray for me and for all my enemies.

243. To love You, Lord Jesus, to love You, to talk to You, to walk with You, to be with You... the rest is vanity.

244. Remember, my son, that temptations are there to be defeated, not to fall into them.

245. At the point of falling, and the Lord hears my sobs. Crying over my sins, sobbing asking for help, groaning... Come to my aid, Lord, lest I perish. I am at the point of becoming a child of the devil.

---

[234] Cf. Ps 118:11.

Come, Lord Jesus! The enemy surrounds me. May they fall in the trap, become prisoners in the net.[235] I, united to You, will be safe. Woe is me! Woe is me, for I love sin more than You! Thank you, Lord, for being able to cry.

246. He carries in his heart all men, their groans, their anguishes. He carries in his heart the indifference of so many in the Church toward the groans of the people who, far from God, suffer in the hell of their sick ego. In the entropy of your love, toward your light, they converge and explode in You, One. My heart receives your light, light from light, fire that pushes me to give my life. To carry all men in one's heart. A thousand universes in You, converging in your light.

247. My father has died. I pray to You for him. Forgive him, take him with You. Through your grace and mercy, I never judged him. I always loved him and felt tenderness toward him. You, my God, gave me understanding and love for him. He was my father; he gave me life. You have granted me to care for him in his last days. I saw him humble and holy. After having confessed and received the anointing of the sick, he asked forgiveness of our mother and all of us. The filial love that you've placed in me surprises and amazes me. It's a love that leads one not to judge, to forgive, to love. It's surprising.

---

[235] Cf. Ps 57:7.

Where does it come from? From You, my God, who are my Father and our Father.[236]

248. Today, October 4, 1994, feast day of St. Francis of Assisi.
Your grace visits me, fills me with your mercy. I will stop watching television; I will deny myself, trusting in You. You help me; You sustain me; You save me. With You, everything goes forward. Everything is rubbish, so that I may gain You, Lord Jesus.[237] St. Francis, intercede for me. The demons have mocked me too much.[238] Now I will humiliate them with humility. The humble maiden of Nazareth helps me. Pray for me.

249. The enemy has closed in and laid siege to me. His traps on every side... And I, weaker and weaker. I will shout, "Save me, Lord!"[239] Don't allow them to defeat me. I deserve to fall for my negligence, but You, Lord, through your great goodness, remember that You are mercy itself. Save me! You are the Holy One. Help me, You who live in the praises of Israel![240] Help me! Come to my aid. Have pity. A thousand demons surround me." Depart

---

[236] Cf. Jn 20:17.
[237] Cf. Phil 3:8.
[238] Cf. Ps 123:3-4.
[239] Cf. Ps 7:2; 70:2; 116:4.
[240] Cf. Ps 22:3.

from me, evil ones! The Lord listens to my lamentations. The Lord hears my prayer.[241]

250. Oh, holy humility of Christ, who could find you! In You alone is true rest. In You alone rests the grace of the Holy Spirit.

251. Who am I? I and my history. The History of Salvation is the Word of God that is made flesh in the womb of the Holy Virgin Mary. Only Christ is the Word made flesh,[242] History made flesh. He is the History of Salvation. In Him there is no past. I am myself plus the history that God is doing with me. I am saved in the Word; I live in Him.
The devil wants me to leave the History of Salvation, he wants me to build my own history, outside of God, he wants me to make my own cosmogony, he wants me to be like God. There is only one history. It is in Christ. He is the Alpha and the Omega.[243] He is everything. He is God.

252. What is the way that leads to heaven? Humility. What is the path that crosses the rugged mountain full of dangers? Humility.

253. Why do I not accept injustice? Because I am not humble.

---

[241] Cf. Ps 66:19.
[242] Cf. Jn 1:14.
[243] Cf. Rev. 1:8.

254. The tree raised up on high, the tree of life, is the cross, is humility. Without humility, there is nothing. There is no place where one loves more than on the cross, together with Him, united to Him.

255. Do not consider yourself more highly than what you are: a hypocrite, a sinner, total impediment, useless servant,[244] useless. Over my uselessness, His strength. Over my falseness, His love as for Judas. Over my sins, His constant forgiveness. Over me, his love and mercy. Give me, Lord, humility and love for You above all things.

256. We made a trip to Asia and Oceania: Manila (meeting with 12,000 youth; 370 stood up to enter the seminary and 300 girls to enter convents), Sydney, Perth, Japan, Hong Kong, Malaysia (Kota Kinabalu), Singapore, Seoul, Pusan, Taiwan (Kaohsiung), Macau, China (Shangchuan Island where St. Francis Xavier died), Hong Kong again, Singapore, and back. Almost 40 days. At times totally exhausted. Visiting seminaries, having meetings with bishops and priests, meeting the brothers of the communities.

The "economic boom" surprised us, the new reality: the same skyscrapers everywhere, people dressed the same; it's the "monoculture." The secularization is arriving that puts the pagan religions in crisis and prepares the peoples for the

---

[244] Cf. Lk 17:10.

announcement of the Gospel. In many peoples and religions, the catalyst is Nature, with its cycles, its storms, its illnesses, etc. In the great secularized cities, the new catalyst, instead, is History.

In Christ, alive and in action, religion is surpassed: "God will be worshiped neither on Mount Gerizim nor on the mount of Jerusalem. The true worshippers the Father seeks are coming, those who worship in Spirit and truth."[245]

The Catholic Church has had a council that has laid the foundation for a true renewal, facing the third millennium. In front of secularization, the Church strips herself, so to speak, of the garment of cyclical, natural religion, and announces the Gospel from a new vantage point: Eternal life within us! We may love beyond death, be *one* in the other. Our ties and slaveries to vices and concupiscence, to honor, selfishness, money... have been broken. Our debts have been paid. God gives us his nature. God adopts us as his children. We have risen with Christ. We no longer die! The Spirit of God lives in us.

257. Whenever God appears, beforehand I am humiliated. An angel precedes Him who obliges me to bend down, to prostrate myself: The Lord is coming! Also, so that I do not glorify myself, so that I do not appropriate for myself what comes from God. In this trip to Asia, before each visit to a nation, there are always sufferings, crises with

---

[245] Cf. Jn 4:21,23.

Carmen, tiredness, etc. After feeling defeated, broken, with my sins and with the feeling of being a total impediment, came the intervention of the Lord: the communities, the priests, the seminaries, the bishop, etc. Impressive passage of God with his consolation and gentleness. We leave consoled, are about to reach another nation, and again crisis, sins, arguments, sufferings, tiredness, fights, etc. The greater the sufferings, the greater the glory afterward. In the end, glory to the Lord! I am an unworthy being; I hope you do not remove your grace from me lest I become incapable of evangelizing. Sometimes with Carmen *I can't take it anymore,* but You help me. I understand that Carmen is totally necessary for the mission.

258. February 1995.
Everything is difficult. Without feelings, with a weakened faith, at the point of thinking You are abandoning me, very tired, nothing gratifies me, sometimes with an immense desire to sin.... Only the zeal of your love for men and the possibility to do them good sustains me. But the devil tells me it's my neurosis, that it is not true love. It's true that I am not Christian. Lord, have mercy. Help me! Where shall I go? Do not leave me, Lord. Come to my aid.[246]
We're going to Spain, to begin a convivence. I have no desire to do so. Again, fights with Carmen, sufferings, talking, talking. We have to listen to

---

[246] Cf. Ps 22:20.

about 100 brothers, and I have no energy. Have I reached the end? No! You will help me. You sustain me, you defend me, you renew me with your grace. You save me from the devil and his traps. I am afraid, Lord. Help me! Put a little love for You in my heart. I feel alone and the devil invites me to go look for a woman who understands me and loves me… Carmen, from morning to night, beats me and corrects me: that I don't pray, that I'm vain, that I do everything myself, etc. Thanks to her, perhaps, I may not be condemned. She has more zeal than I, prays more than I, is better than I in everything. I am a disaster and I feel tempted to leave everything and go who knows where… Lord, come, I am alone, alone! Come. Already 30 years have gone by without stopping for an instant. Help me. I am afraid that a terrible persecution may come, calumnies. You have always been so good, and I have repaid You badly. I have put your work in danger. To know myself like this destroys me inside. Have mercy, Lord, for my soul will be lost. You, only You. I have nothing besides my sins. Love me, Lord! Console me. Do not allow me to leave You. A thousand demons surround me; in the name of the Lord, I will defeat them.[247]

259. *To be consummated in your will.*
Exhausted, without strength…
with the happiness of dying,

---

[247] Cf. Ps 118:11-12.

a total foreigner in this world.
Tired.
And to go on, to go on
surrounded by a thousand temptations,
with no consolation,
alone and afraid.
Lord! You take pity on me.
My Jesus,
to love you and continue
as long as I can…
Come, help me!
Come Lord, console me.
Jesus, my love…
Come!

260. *O Lord, our God,*
my soul thirsts for You;
my heart longs for You;
my body, my skin,
like dry land, longs for You.[248]
Do not abandon me, Lord!
Abandonment, loneliness,
fear, tiredness,
inability…
And You, how much longer?[249]

---

[248] Cf. Ps 63:1.
[249] Cf. Ps 6:4.

261. To crucify my reason in the unreasonableness. In Carmen's constant errors of judgment, in my opinion… To be annihilated in, according to me, the "madness" of the reasons of the other. What is happening to me that I cannot go on? Trust that You will help me. Have mercy on me, Lord. Do not take away my hope in You. Help Carmen.

262. *In this night that burns me.*
In this constant groaning.
In these pitiful sighs over your absence.
"Oh, who can heal me…!"[250]
This pain in my side.
This weight that I feel on my chest.
In this desire to cry
tears of blood.
In this life that is gone.
In this today that is pain.
Oh! "Oh, who can heal me!
Now surrender yourself truly;
no longer send me…"[251]
That dark messenger
who afflicts me inside,
that angel from You who denounces me,
who invades me…
"Oh, who can heal me!…
if in those silver-plated faces of yours
formed suddenly…"[252]

---

[250] St. John of the Cross, *Spiritual Canticle*.
[251] Ibid.
[252] Ibid.

Oh! Oh!... Who could walk with you,
O Lord,
and contemplate the indifference!
And I can't go on any longer! Lord!
Heal me, console me,
love me. Come!

263. *In my chest, Lord,*
You have opened a hole.
It is a dark abyss,
a universe longing for You.
In it I lose myself and suffer.
Oh! Oh!
And these depths of my being unite
with the galaxies.
Into these abysmal depths,
infinite and black, I fall
and I vanish into You.
Do not abandon me,
do not leave me, Lord. Come!
I am left with nothing,
only sins... and You.
Help me, have mercy on me!
Help me, be Yourself and save me.

264. March 19, 1995: to St. Joseph
Husband of the Holy Virgin Mary,
father of the Son of God, and saintly,
chosen as a man, righteous and chaste,
to give the family to the world,
Joseph, image of the Father,

Joseph, righteous, humble and good,
to you we entrust
the families of the world
in which faith can grow,
in which the child becomes an adult,
with the Mother of God,
with the father of Christ.
Holy "families of Nazareth,"
pray to St. Joseph.

265. The poor are evangelized.[253] So many poor people, who are poor in culture, in education, in age. You, Lord, gather them in a community and carry them on your shoulders. Your shoulders are Christ who bears their sins, our sins, for years of forgiveness. My songs, my painting, my time, my life, for them. Putting up with Carmen for You and for them: convivences, convivences, thousands of meetings and convivences; not living for myself. With people who are, humanly speaking, ugly, old, uncultured, and what is worse, tacky... My God, what am I saying? I am worse than all of them in everything. You gave me everything for them. They are your children. You gave your life for them. I am a miserable sinner, worse than everyone. If they knew that I am a wretch, a hypocrite, a sinner... I can't take it anymore! With you, I can go on. Your grace sustains me. You hold me with your love.

---

[253] Cf. Lk 7:22.

266. Following in your footprints.[254] Rejoicing in being humiliated. Following Christ. Seeking his glory. One ascends by descending. His glory is experienced in humiliating oneself. The resurrection is lived on the cross, entering the cross. O glorious cross of the risen Jesus! Oh, holy humility of Christ, who could find you!

267. Love for man produces beauty. Demanding, enslaving, obliging, these destroy beauty. Sin produces horror. Evil is ugly. Where there is ugliness, there is no love. Filth, ugliness, sloppiness, disorder, misery, the smell of garbage, raggedy children, urine, dirty prostitutes, drugs, drunkards, gambling... are the horrible fruits of sin, which is the absence of God, the absence of the crucified Love. I was there, and I felt small.

268. Blessed be your name, Lord. Blessed be your tenderness and mercy. Holy, holy, holy! Heaven and earth are full of your glory. Hosanna! Hosanna! He comes on the meek and humble colt...[255] to set earth aflame. Blazing fire that consumes my soul.
My spirit burns, burns in You, my God. My heart groans at the sight of your Name being vilified and man exploited, beaten, cheated, in a society that wants to crucify you again,[256] to destroy the last

---

[254] Cf. 1 P 2:21.
[255] Cf. Jn 12:15.
[256] Cf. Heb 6:6.

vestiges of Christian faith. Superstition, magic, idolatry. Modesty is being killed in the youth. Abortion, homosexuality, free sex. Everything holy is insulted and presented as harmful. The devil climbs the ladder, wants to seat himself in heaven to be adored as a god. "I saw Satan fall from heaven like a bolt of lightning..."[257] To evangelize. "Go, I send you like sheep amongst wolves. Bring nothing for the journey.[258] "Look at the fields: they are ripe for the harvest... I send you to collect what you have not sown."[259]

With the fire of the Spirit of God in the heart, which wants the maximum good for all people, and the blood of Jesus fallen into the furrow of history for the salvation of all, alive.

Water, blood, fire, Baptism, Eucharist, Spirit. The grace of your Spirit that gives itself totally. "*Os-di*", "*Di-os*".[260] God has given us. Your Spirit burns me, obliges me to give myself, drags me in this self-giving, in this being Eucharist, bread that is broken and given. Blood that is poured out, fire of love that sears me with the desire for the blood and flesh to be valid for all, for the sacrifice of God to arrive to man.

---

[257] Cf. Lk 10:18.
[258] Cf. Lk 10:3-4.
[259] Jn 4:35,38.
[260] A play on the Spanish word for God, where the two syllables of the word God (Di-os) are reversed in order to mean "I gave you", (Os-di).

They must be fed.[261] His Body must be brought to the multitude gathered in small communities of 50 and 100.[262] "Give them something to eat... There is a boy here with five loaves and two fish."[263] This boy is Israel, which has been given the five loaves, the Torah, and the two fish, the Sabbath. Israel had the Torah, the way of truth that leads to rest, to repose, and the two fish (double ration of manna that is collected on Friday, the two fish).[264]

This young man gives Christ the Torah, *the way* that leads to the *true rest (Sabbath)*, so that He may travel it. Christ makes us sit down in groups of 50 and of 100, and He gives us the bread and fish fulfilled in Him, the Torah and the Sabbath fulfilled in his Body and in his Blood. He is the Passover[265] that brings us into heaven.

To break the bread. Multiply the loaves. The Torah was waiting for him. When it feels the Jesus' hands on it, it multiplies, it is realized, it fulfils its mission. It satisfies! It gives itself.

Who can understand these books? And the heavens cried, and no one was able to open the seven seals. Where is the wounded Lamb? The Lamb that bleeds?[266]

---

[261] Cf. Mt 14:16.
[262] Cf. Mk 6:40.
[263] Cf. Mk 6:37; Jn 6:9.
[264] Cf. Ex 16:22.
[265] Cf. 1 Cor 5:7.
[266] Cf. Rev. 5:1-10.

The multitude, the desert, the fatigue, so many days without meat. A young man gives Christ the five loaves and two fish. "'Have them sit'... There was a large field of grass..."[267] "To meadows of green grass he leads us."[268]

Amid the paganism that makes my heart groan, that burns my entrails, the consolation of the Gospel, of your Word: "Who will be able to feed this multitude in the desert?"[269] To satiate man with You, my God. Inebriated with your blood, with your love.

269. Today, January 7, 1996, I am returning to these pages after a long time.

A few days ago, I had an audience with the Holy Father, just he and I.

I saw him tired and suffering. I had the impression that the flow of the day, with its inexorable duty, was for him a constant crucifixion. Each audience, each meeting... he goes like a meek lamb to the cross of Christ. "A giant in faith," great fruit for the Church. In his breast, a rock of love for Christ and for all people.

I told him how I urgently felt the necessity for the Church to recover the celebration of the Word,[270] because the mass media is in the hands of the world. The *kerygma*... etc. He told me, "Of course. In the world there is the 'anti-word.'"

---

[267] Cf. Jn 6:10.
[268] Cf. Ps 23:2.
[269] Cf. Jn 6:5-7; Ps 78:19-20.
[270] Cf. *Caeremoniale Episcoporum*, No. 226.

270. The one who leaves men to find God, encounters men in God.

271. The one who leaves God for men is always divided.

272. Today, January 9, 1996.
I am 57 years old today. I'm headed for St. Catherine's Monastery in Sinai.
I think about my mother, who is in the hospital in Madrid. I was born during the Spanish Civil War. My father was on the frontlines. My mother told me that when I was born it seemed like someone was hitting her with an iron rod in the kidneys, that she will never forget it. Poor thing! Help her, Lord! Have mercy on me, who am unworthy, a sinner, a hypocrite. Above my nothingness, You. I was created for You and am in You, only in you, who are who You are. The fire of the burning bush[271] in my heart. In the heart of the Church. From Mount Sinai to the Promised Land, a process, a way: from Pentecost to heaven. A fire that consumes all that is not. The bush full of thorns. It burns. Fire of the love of God in the heart of the Church, little bush, full of thorns, that never burns out, that is not consumed, the fire of the love of God that rains on the good and the bad.[272] "Fire that rains."[273] Fire that makes us one with all, fire that consumes the sin that divides us from ourselves and others.

---

[271] Cf. Ex 3:2.
[272] Cf. Mt 5:45.
[273] Cf. Ex 24:17.

273. My mother is dying... And I give you thanks, Lord, for being able to be with her. My mother, tiny and suffering, but always full of faith and strength. Help her, Lord!

274. Persecution is a grace. It permits us to love as God loves. You don't light a lamp except to put it on a stand.[274] What is the light? The love of God in us, the divine nature shown in the cross of Christ: God loving his enemies to the point of death. This divine essence, this love, is light.

    God loves us totally, even if we hate him, even when we are evil... He loves us to the point of death, gives himself completely for us. If He is inside of us, if he has given us his very nature, the way this light is seen, and shines, is to put it on the lampstand, which is the cross of persecution, the cross of the enemies. They are a grace. They make us resemble Christ. Through them, faith is shown to the world. The enemies who hate Christ today are redeemed, so to speak, by the love shown to them in not resisting their evil, offering for their salvation the suffering of the cross they inflict on you, completing in history what is lacking in the passion of Christ.[275] "Love your enemies... Do not resist evil..."[276] Persecution is a grace. It saves us because it makes us resemble Christ crucified.

---

[274] Cf. Mt 5:15.
[275] Cf. Col 1:24.
[276] Mt 5:39,44.

275. I am in Vienna. We came from Berlin. In Bonn, Chancellor Kohl received us. Everything went very well. God helps us in everything. His mercy is infinite, immense, overwhelming. I... a hypocrite, a traitor, fake, a Pharisee... the last and worst of all. It sounds cliché, and yet it's the truth. My total weakness, my innumerable sins... your love and holiness... Forgive me, Lord! Have compassion, for I will repay you.[277] You have chosen me to do a work that so many times I despise... Cover over my sins. Help Carmen. She is suffering. Have mercy on me. The seminaries... the Church, the world, secularization, paganism, illnesses, old age, death... And You... You alone are total love, given totally. Placed there, in the tabernacle. To the point of death, for everyone. Your blood fell in the furrow of our life and sowed your love forever.

276. If only I could mortify myself... I cannot; I am like a paralytic. And the resplendent light of your love... Is it that you do not want me to think I am holy lest I be full of pride and arrogance? Behold me. A sinner. The last and worst of all. A thousand graces from your love, and I... a hypocrite. I preach what I do not do. Have mercy on me, Lord.
Your total love renews me, washes me, forgives me. I already feel love for everyone. Let us hurry and save Europe. It is your blood that has filled our poor husks with elation and joy. Let's go out to the

---

[277] Cf. Mt 18:26.

streets, the villages and towns, to the villas, the hamlets and cities. For Christ is risen!

277. God is love.[278] The Universe is full of his love. If our actions are not love, if they are outside of God's will, they are nothing... The devil chains us to them through vice. Christ breaks our chains and frees us. Works of life.

278. Woe to the man whose fame is greater than his works! Woe is me!

279. "Love and do what whatever you will..."[279] If you have *zeal*, love for man, love for the Church ("zeal for your house consumes me"[280]), this love, this zeal, this fire, makes you innocent. Innocence makes you an offering pleasing to God, who listens to you and obeys you. "Everything is possible for the one who believes."[281] From zeal, innocence is born, from innocence, ritual sacrifice, from ritual sacrifice, self-control, from self-control, holiness.[282] The prophet has zeal for God, which makes him love mankind to the end. "Love bears everything, excuses everything...."[283] Love, and everything becomes possible for you. You love because God gave you his Spirit and the fire of his love purified

---

[278] Cf. 1 Jn 4:8,16.
[279] Cf. St. Augustine, *Homily on First Letter of John* 7,8.
[280] Cf. Ps 69:9; Jn 2:17.
[281] Cf. Mk 9:23.
[282] Cf. *Mishnah, Sotah*, 9:15.
[283] Cf. 1 Cor 13:7.

you and made of you the perfectly innocent one: "Christ," the only holy lamb who takes away the sins of the world,[284] the new Moses, who speaks face to face with God, the perfect image of God, equal to God, true God. God from God, light from light, true God from true God.[285]

"I can do all things in Him who gives me strength."[286] Faith that makes you stand firm as if you were beholding the Invisible One, like Moses.[287] Faith and Charity united are like the fire that penetrates iron and melts it in a white light that hopes for everything: heavenly Hope. Three virtues that come from God: Faith, Hope, and Charity. Theological, supernatural virtues, that produce in us the four cardinal virtues: prudence (discernment), justice (of God, the thirst for divine justice,[288] the justice of the cross in everything), fortitude (total patience) and temperance (self-control, constant death of the ego). Zeal. Innocence. Sacrifice. Purification or self-control. Holiness.

Love and conquer, because God is love.[289]

280. We are in Istanbul. May 6, 1996.

Yesterday at twelve the Orthodox Patriarch received us, his All Holiness Bartholomew I. I read

---

[284] Cf. Jn 1:29.
[285] Cf. *Nicene Creed*.
[286] Cf. Phil 4:13.
[287] Cf. Heb 11:27.
[288] Cf. Mt 5:6.
[289] Cf. 1 Jn 4:8,16.

him part of the letter I wrote to the Pope about the new anthropology and Babylon, the culture of the "Great City."[290] He received us well, listened attentively and put us in contact with a deacon appointed by him to follow up with us, for a possible collaboration with the Way.

Istanbul is a good example of what is happening all over the world. The number of young people who are abandoning religion (Islam) and stroll about the streets dressed like Europeans is impressive. The Christian churches are almost empty, and many are closed. The streets are packed... and the zeal for your house consumes me.[291] The two Neocatechumenal communities here, in the parish of St. Anthony, are full of young couples. All enthusiastic. They welcomed us as if they were welcoming Christ. It is hopeful. They have been in the Way for ten years and are much stronger than at the beginning. The religious order tolerates us. The pastor, Fr. Luis, an Italian from Pescara, a saint. Thanks to him, a door has opened in Turkey.

Istanbul, the ancient Byzantium, Constantinople... The mosques... Everything passes. Today, 11 million inhabitants, a ton of cars, movies, television, modern life, hamburgers and America... Full speed toward the destruction of the family, abortion, no more children, suicides among the youth... Secularization, modern life... And You, Lord, my

---

[290] Cf. Rev. 11:8.
[291] Cf. Ps 69:9; Jn 2:17.

God, who love all men! This is a wonderful moment to evangelize. It is the *"Kairos* of God": religion is being surpassed and the modern world is opening itself to faith realized in history. The wall has fallen, the *iconostasis*. The Lord has prepared a table for us in the midst of the desert.[292] People of the East, stand up, for the Lord is coming to save you! He comes to you meek and humble of heart![293] Thousands of young people shout: Hosanna! Hosanna! Blessed is he who comes in the name of the Lord![294]

281. The sin that lives in our flesh causes us to experience the emptiness of our being. Separated from God, it has no support and we become fascinated by "things." In them we are seeking God, without knowing it. We seek to be loved, we seek to "be", that is, to live. Money, fame, order, culture, sexuality, to be loved… A thousand mirrors shattered and shining, without unity, prisoners of a thousand vices… Without support. You, my rock![295] Thousands of young people in the streets. And zeal for your house consumes me.[296] You can touch the deepest part of their being. With faith, you can heal their minds, give them the true vision of things, the light of the History of their

---

[292] Cf. Ps 78:19.
[293] Cf. Mt 21:5.
[294] Cf. Mt 21:9.
[295] Cf. Ps 18:2; 94:22.
[296] Cf. Ps 69:9; Jn 2:17.

history. Give them salvation, give them Eternal Life. Send the Church!

282. Four new *Redemptoris Mater* seminaries have been born. Blessed be God! Manila, with Cardinal Sin, who requested it. Managua, with Cardinal Obando Bravo. Douala (Cameroon), with Cardinal Tumi, Karaganda (Kazakhstan). We sent 750 youth two by two throughout Europe, 10 days, without money, to announce the Gospel in the parishes. Everyone returned with the light of the risen Christ in their eyes. Many went hungry. Others had to sleep in the streets with the poor. All were able to suffer a little for Christ and offer it for the Church. Total obedience, profound communion, joy, etc., all this is your work, Humble, Holy, Blessed.

283. *Your reflection,*
beauty contained
in that mathematical architrave.
Everything held together by your love,
sustained…
And my body and my being?
For without You, it cannot…
For without You, I do not want to live.
Oh, what pain,
when the soul is extinguished!
The mathematical content
of the cosmic architrave
is stilled
and departs… dead.

284. *Why do I die without You?*
Why does life lose its meaning?
Who brought me here
without asking me?
Who exposed me
and left me naked?
He who called me
from the depths of my being.
He who did not let my soul be lost,
who did not let it leave the earthen vessel of that body
that blindly sought its content…
Always your wounded eyes
in so many poor people…
Your eyes?
Of whom am I enamored? Of what?
And why do I stray from the path?
For that mule
slowly climbs the slope.
And scattered all around
is Your beauty.
How I would love to see You,
my Jesus; with You
I am in love, only with You,
and only upon my soul do I live.
For she is my ship that sails
upon the impassive waves of my days.

285. You have predestined, prepared some good works for me beforehand, so that I might walk in them, so that I might carry them out, says St. Paul.²⁹⁷
I must discover them little by little following your footprints:²⁹⁸ Meekness, humility, sweetness, discernment... Lord Jesus, have mercy on me. I am full of weakness, sins; I am a hypocrite. How will I be saved? Have mercy on me. Your grace, your constant, gracious love, without resentment, full of compassion, visits me every morning and invites me to begin anew.

286. We have been "created in Christ Jesus, for the good works which God has already designated to make up our way of life."²⁹⁹
The "good work" of God is:
- first, to be united to Him by constant remembrance ("hesychia"³⁰⁰);
- second, interior silence in Him;
- third, constant prayer, prostration, the psalms, the liturgy;
- fourth, spiritual reading;
- fifth, to cry over one's sins and to remember the Passion of Christ;

---

²⁹⁷ Cf. Eph 2:10.
²⁹⁸ Cf. 1 P 2:21.
²⁹⁹ Eph 2:10. *New Jerusalem Bible.*
³⁰⁰ A spiritual state of union with God, recollection, interior silence, tranquility, peace, repose, etc. "Come to Me all you who labor and are overburdened... *and you will find rest for your souls*" (Mt 11:28-29).

- sixth, the constant remembrance of God and death;
- seventh, the holy humility of Christ; in it one finds the true "stillness."

To achieve this, first you must renounce the world, its vanity, its pleasures and lies, loving Christ above all things.

"Wake up sleeper, arise from the dead, and Christ will shine on you,"[301] and you will attain Christ.

287. We climbed Mount Sinai to receive a Statute: "*Shema*, Israel…"[302] This Word was fulfilled in Christ. He is our *Shema*. We receive him thanks to Baptism that seals us in the Holy Spirit.

At dawn, after having walked all night, we arrived at the summit and sang Lauds. The Word of the Office of Readings of that day "by chance" was Deuteronomy 6, the *Shema*. A special touch of love from the Lord amid persecutions and work, pressures, and anguishes.

They want us to make a Statute of the Way, and we don't know if they want to transform us into a religious congregation, an association or something like that. They can do with us what they like… The Lord, who is our strength,[303] will help us. "Do not resist evil."[304]

The Church, the Curia, the Pope, the bishops, have always helped us. Why doubt now? Christ is alive.

---

[301] Eph 5:14.
[302] Cf. Mk 12:29.
[303] Cf. Ps 28:7-8.
[304] Mt 5:39.

He is risen. If he wants to die again with us to show his glory… Blessed be his name. May He give us strength. For my part, the only thing I want is not to sin. And to love Jesus, to love him, because I love him very little. Virgin Mary, help me!

288. Giorgio Filippucci died: married, with 10 children, expecting the 11th. An itinerant catechist, responsible for the Way in Umbria (Italy). He sang the *Shema*, a song he composed, on the summit of Mount Sinai. While praying Lauds with his team, after the time of silent prayer, going to give the sign of peace to the priest, his aorta ruptured, and he died on the spot. 20 years itinerant with his whole family. He was a nuclear engineer. One of the youngest of those who went up the mountain. Lord, may he be with You. Filippucci, pray for me.

289. Resurrection Sunday, 1997.
I feel like the women who go to the tomb. Where is my Lord? Where have you placed him? Someone stole him from my soul… Who will roll away the stone? Lord, help me.[305]
More than 270 bishops from the Americas, from North to South, have signed up for the convivence of bishops in New York. We begin next Tuesday. I am afraid. Lord, help me! My Jesus, my Jesus, do not leave me. I am a wretch. Have mercy. Christ is risen! Who will announce it to me? Who will console

---

[305] Cf. Mk 16:3; Jn 20:15.

me? Who will give me the Good News? May someone knock on my door and tell me on behalf of the Lord that Christ is risen for me, that the Kingdom of God has arrived, that my sins have been forgiven. Alleluia!

290. August 1997.
Lord, help me to unite faith to virtue, to virtue, spiritual reading, to be temperate (which I am incapable of), to have patience (above all with myself and with all my defects), to pray (which I do very little), to have love for my neighbors. Above all, give me "Charity," which is the love that comes from You.

291. December 1997.
I am a wretch, a sinner. Lord, do not hand me over to my enemies. Have mercy!

They push me toward the void.
They deceive me, they throw me...
And in the void
is the hell of your absence.
Without You and without dying.
What a horror!
An empty universe.
On a cold night
my dull spirit,
suspended in the void
toward Hell.
And in the air, the implacable demons

who await me.
The shell of everything that exists
decomposes and turns to naught.
Art, the harmony of your love,
which holds everything together,
has gone and... dust, nothingness.

Lord Jesus, forgive me! Help me. I don't deserve anything, but You are merciful, infinite mercy. On the cross, your compassion. You, the only one who knows about evil and death...

292. I am painting the "*Dormitio*" in Florence. January 1998. I just turned 59 and You...

293. Meeting with the Orthodox in Moscow. The Lord always accompanies us. His love for us is so good and gentle. Zeal for your house. The Neocatechumenal communities of Moscow, Hilarion (the Hegumen)... and loving You, Lord Jesus.
We offered them the Way. They asked for a written document of what it might look like. Lord, if it comes from You, help us.

294. Today is Holy Thursday, 1998.
I am being left with nothing. Without prayer, without faith, in total weakness, as if the bandages of Lazarus enveloped me once more. It's as though I must lose my soul. My God have mercy!
Woe is me, for I preach poverty, but always have money in my pockets!

Woe is me, for I am incapable of mortifying myself in anything!

Woe is me, for I do not practice what I preach![306] Lord, help me!

Woe is me, my eyes always full of lust!

Woe is me, for making others walk, I am myself about to be disqualified![307]

Woe is me! Who will be able to heal me…! And in this evil of absences must I patiently accept seeing myself walk toward the abyss?

Woe is me, for I want to love, and I do the opposite! I don't move, shackled, full of pain. With nothing. You have done thousands of miracles with me, and I a sinner and a traitor, cowardly and treacherous.

Woe is me, for I lie, and I don't care… I pretend! And for what?

"Oh, who has the power to heal me?
Now wholly surrender yourself!
Do not send me
any more messengers;
they cannot tell me what I must hear…
How do you endure
O life, not living where you live,
and being brought near death
by the arrows you receive
from that which you conceive of your Beloved?[308]

---

[306] Cf. Mt 23:3.
[307] Cf. 1 Cor 9:27.
[308] St. John of the Cross, *Spiritual Canticle*.

Woe is me, for my fame is greater than my works!
Woe is me, for I am walking toward Gehenna!
Woe is me, for I barely pray!
Woe is me, for I am left only with your absence and its pain!
Save me, Lord, I implore you! Have mercy! Help me. Nothing matters to me, only loving You… The devil roars, prowls around, circles me, seeking to devour me.[309] The Holy Virgin helps me. Holy Mary, pray for me. What is happening to me? Who is binding me? Who is it that is blindfolding me? Get out! Get out! Lord, help me!

295. Be careful, Kiko, for success and praise lead to pride. Failures and humiliations lead to humility. Pride destroys everything in the soul. How horrible the empty soul is, without God, in hell. What terrifying suffering without You.

296. *I can do without everything,*
except You,
lest I die.
I have a light inside my soul
that, when I look around,
illuminates things with its light.
People rush past,
and I look at them with your light,
and my heart burns
to help them.

---

[309] Cf. 1 P 5:8.

If the light in my soul is extinguished...
Beauty died
and an old, drunken vagabond
hobbled by, staggering,
who left and never returned.

297. A culture of not suffering envelops us, of worship of the body, of the worship of nature; herbs, filters, massages, animals, magic rites, the Amazon, the East... sex, money, feeling good, wellness, not suffering... Who is teaching us to live like this? Who invites us to detest the cross of Christ and our own cross? How can we escape a hedonistic and lying culture that leads to suicide and euthanasia, that makes us detest old age? They bury us in deceptions. And millions suffocate and die. Everywhere full of divorces, boys and girls broken like dolls no longer good to play with... Young people wounded in the deepest part of their being. Who will bring Christ to you? Who will bind your wounds, heal you inside and give you back what is yours,[310] what the thieves of the soul stole from you?[311] Who deceived your parents so that they would separate and bite your soul with their teeth? The wolves of Hell. The hatred, the screaming... and they get divorced and don't care about anything. If you die...

---

[310] Cf. Lk 16:12.
[311] Cf. Lk 10:30,36.

298. Without beauty, we could not live. Through it we receive an aesthetic emotion, an "anonymous" pleasure that "someone" procures for us. In the beauty of creation, *You* are there, loving us. The harmony of light that caresses things and ordains them for good. Light, color, mathematical order that distributes space, surfaces, in a texture that is always organized aesthetically; distinct shapes of inexhaustible, overflowing genius surround us: You are there like a canvas that invites the soul to pass beyond it.

We can lack many things, but not beauty. In it we realize that "someone" *wants us to fall in love with him*. He does beautiful things for us because he loves us. It surprises us that someone should love us. He loves us and we don't know why. Grace frightens us, what is given for free terrorizes us, we would like to buy aesthetics. Beauty invites us to contemplation and abandonment, ecstasy, and being one with another frightens us.

Love attracts us and scares us. Transcending ourselves in that which is totally other. The mathematical formula of everything beautiful, the light, sound, history... that invites me to abandon myself... to believe in the love of Someone who loves me, without forcing me. Beauty surrounds the "Word," Christ. In it, He speaks and invites me to believe. Only faith cures my mind of pride, transfigures it and permits me to see the truth: God exists!

299. *Help me, Lord*
 to not doubt You,
 To never doubt your love.
 Your grace, pouring out,
 left my heart already blooming
 With a thousand desires of love,[312]
 for I can do no more than suffer,
 Than live, groaning.
 And in this dark flame of your love,
 In this veil that envelops
 my soul and stifles it,
 I feel my heart dislocate,
 open, and pour itself out
 like water flooding your garden.

300. I am stunned at your holiness over my sinful being. Your love appears over me and destroys me, stuns me, crucifies me… I am terrified. I expect Hell and your love appears and terrorizes me, stuns me… Oh, Lord, have pity on me!

301. Each humiliation a Christian receives is a grace.

302. Year 1999.
 We are in the Ginosar Kibbutz, near Tiberias, on the shore of the lake. You will help us.

303. We have laid the first stone of the *Domus Galilaeae*. The Latin Patriarch of Jerusalem, Michel Sabbah,

---

[312] Cf. St. John of the Cross, *Spiritual Canticle*.

came, accompanied by his auxiliary bishops and bishops from other rites: Melkite, Armenian, Syrian, Greek Orthodox, etc., and also the nuncio, and religious men and women of the Holy Land: the Benedictines of Tabgha, the Dominicans from the *Ecole Biblique*, the Franciscans who gave us the land, some Salesians... members of Focolare and of other movements, and the Hebrew civil authorities from Upper Galilee. It was a true event, something important happened. The Lord was present.

And I... a wretch who denies Jesus Christ. I have a devil who throws me to the ground so that I don't glorify myself[313] whenever God does a miracle. *Everything is yours.* Mine are the sins. Help me, Lord! Convert me to You. Save me, for I shall be condemned! Holy Virgin, Virgin Mary, pray for me. My Holy Mother, help me!

304. Divine foolishness is wiser than all human wisdom, and divine weakness stronger than all the power of men.[314] Your weakness in me facing the power, the powers of the world. Your weakness in me, without offering resistance, offering the other cheek[315] (what foolishness for the world), accepting to be captured, calumniated, without offering resistance ("do not resist evil"[316]), allowing oneself to be beaten, whipped, tortured, crucified (what weakness,

---

[313] Cf. 2 Cor 12:7.
[314] Cf. 1 Cor 1:25.
[315] Cf. Mt 5:39.
[316] Cf. Mt 5:39.

how absurd). "Divine weakness is stronger than men." He was weak to the point of allowing himself to be killed. There is nothing stronger than death.... In his weakness, he overcame death. Eternal life, which was with the Father, was made manifest.[317]

305. Lord, have mercy on me, for I am a sinner! Help me, for I cannot do it any longer. Give me faith and understanding to be able to fight against disbelief. Give me wisdom and intelligence to be able to discern the traps of the devil and deny him. Give me temperance, prayer and strength to be able to fight against the passions that surround me wherever I go: they cling to my skin, they penetrate my pores and suffocate my poor soul that groans and sighs for You. Give me purity and vigilance so that I may not sadden your Spirit.[318] Give me humility and meekness so that your friendship and constant dialogue may live in me. Grant me, above all, *not to judge anybody*, for I am impure, vain, proud, false, a liar, fatuous, pompous... I have lost all your treasures. Who could have charity, peace, joy, generosity, goodness, modesty, innocence, patience to suffer injustice looking at You, Lord, my God! Loving You is the only truth; the rest is vanity.

306. We should pay someone to insult us, because You were insulted. We should pay someone to slap us,

---

[317] Cf. 1 Jn 1:2.
[318] Cf. Eph 4:30.

because You were slapped. We should pay to be despised, because You, O Lord, were despised, scoffed at, hated... so hated. And if they insult us, hate us, despise us *for free*, so much the better.

307. *And in this drifting life*
and in this being of You
and of death...
My life passes
like the meek waters of that river.
They run silently
between branches and mountains
and towns and peoples,
and that bridge...
and again the silence,
from the forest a howl.
And I feel in my chest
the pain of You.
The meaning of my life
that passes and passes.
But my being is pressed,
dry of You.
Life drifts,
the river runs,
but with You I am bearing
the world
that penetrates and gets smaller in me.
It all fits...
I am going to China
and God will help me.
March 12, 2000.

308. *My life escapes me*
like water running
through my fingers
(and I don't know what to do).
I would like to hold back life.
I would like it to move slower
(but no...)
It flows and flows and goes away.
And I, I do not ride it.
And I, I do not dominate it.
And I, I do not live it,
It passes above me.
I am already dead...
To live life
without living it,
without drinking it in
(oh, to grow old).
Life is given to me
so that it may be love.
Why has life
fallen out of love with me?
Why do you escape?
Why do you flee?
Wait!
Stop!
So that I may live you.
You depart, oh, life!
And you leave me alone with death.
March 21, 2000.

309. The Lord has been waiting for you on this mountain." Those are the words the Pope said to us after blessing the Sanctuary of the Word in the *Domus Galilaeae*, on the top of the Mount of the Beatitudes. Fifty thousand young people from the Way, with the Pope, opened the third millennium. "Go to Galilee. There you will see me."[319] From the mountain, the risen Jesus sent his disciples to all nations. After 2,000 years, young people from one hundred nations were there with Peter. "From them I will take priests for me, priests to announce my glory."[320] With this fact, the Lord is speaking. "He goes before you to Galilee."[321] "The Lord has been waiting for you..." We have arrived, Lord, what do you want of us? "Do not resist evil. Love your enemies."[322]

Christ crucified is the heavenly man. A new era. A New Evangelization. A time of grace for the Hebrew people. If the gentiles reject Christ, if they vomit him up, sinning against the light, has the hour come to lift the veil God placed over his people in favor of the gentiles?[323] "Go to Galilee – Galilee of the gentiles – There you will see me."[324]

---

[319] Cf. Mt 28:10.
[320] Is 66:19,21.
[321] Cf. Mt 26:32.
[322] Cf. Mt 5:39,44.
[323] Cf. 2 Cor 3:14.
[324] Cf. Mt 28:10

310. Holy Thursday 2000.
I am in Zamora (Spain), in the parish of St. Frontis. It has been 33 years since we came here in the year 1967. We were still in the shantytown. The mustard seed is now a tree in which the birds of the sky are beginning to live.[325]

311. Lord Jesus, to You be the glory forever. Help me! Grant me, Lord, sweetness, simplicity, meekness, patience, humility, mercy. It's your image in my soul. It is you, Lord, living inside me. You are the living one, full of meekness and simplicity, the patient one, humble, sweet and merciful... It is you. Oh, who will be able to love you!

312. Every humiliation is a grace. Every humiliation we receive is written in heaven for our sanctification. They are the luminous footprints of Christ. He, being God, humbled himself and left for us the luminous footprints from his feet so that we may follow him.[326] His steps are eternal, they lead to heaven and save mankind.
Following along the way of Christ, placing our feet in his footsteps.
Footprints full of light, the light of Mt. Tabor, light of the resurrection, light of the life of God in us.
"Insulted, He did not respond with insults, enduring evil. He did not threaten, rather He placed

---

[325] Cf. Mt 13:31-32.
[326] Cf. 1 P 2:21.

Himself in the hands of the one who judges justly..."[327]

Patiently bearing injuries and insults, letting evil and injustice reach our flesh, reach the soul of our tarnished honor, what pain!

The deep imperative of my Baptism is maximum charity, maximum love for others. The whole world with its history is in our hearts, visited by the grace of the Holy Spirit. Our heart only rests in total love for everyone and is fulfilled on the cross with Christ.

Co-redeemers like the Virgin Mary, saviors of the entire universe. Saints, bearing sins, injuries and insults, bearing in our bodies what is lacking in his passion.[328] We are the body of the risen Christ.

To follow Christ along the way, planting our feet in his luminous footprints, to save everyone who must be saved, in Christ, with Christ and for Christ, to Him be honor and glory. Amen.

313. What does it mean to be humble? To bear injuries and insults patiently, seeing in these events the will of God.

314. The world is supported by three things: The Word, the Liturgy, and Charity. He who attacks any of these pillars, puts his life in peril and will leave the

---

[327] Cf. 1 P 2:23.
[328] Cf. Col 1:24.

world. Envy, lust and hatred for one's neighbor call for death.

315. The Way is supported by three things: Word, Liturgy, and *Koinonia* (Community). The Torah, the divine service and works of mercy: these things support the world, as the Fathers of Israel have already said.[329]

316. Word, Liturgy, and Community, holy tripod upon which our Christian life rests.[330] Do not judge,[331] do not fornicate, love as I have loved you…[332] Do not resist evil.[333] Our enemies are given to us so that we may save the world with Christ through Charity. Total love. Christian love. The love of Christ crucified. Work of eternal life that calls the world to faith.

317. Everything in life that makes us resemble Christ crucified is a grace.

318. The enemy is a grace. He is given to you so that you may save the world by loving him. "Love your enemies. Do good to those who hate you. Do not

---

[329] Cf. *Pirkei Avot*, 1,2.
[330] Vatican II mentions this tripod 54 times.
[331] Cf. Mt 7:1.
[332] Cf. Jn 13:24.
[333] Cf. Mt 5:39.

resist evil. When someone strikes you on the right cheek, offer him your left..."[334]

319. Remember, son, that whoever flatters a Christian, hands him over to Satan.

320. Today, the words of the archbishop of Madrid, Archbishop Casimiro Morcillo, referring to our Neocatechumenal communities, come to mind: "I wish that on every street in Madrid there were a Christian community." The community is like the uterus where the seed, the embryo of our Baptismal faith develops and grows. "Father... so that the love with which You have loved me may be in them and I in them."[335] "As You, Father, are in me and I in You, so that they also may be one in us, so that the world might believe that You have sent me."[336]

321. What do you have before you?... You, only You. What does this mean? That before me there is nothing else, no plans, nor fulfillment, nor dreams... Nothing! "Vanity of vanities."[337] "Each day has enough trouble of its own."[338]
To live today in You. Not projecting myself forward, sublimating myself into a thousand chimeras that are false religions, demons,

---

[334] Cf. Mt 5:39,44.
[335] Jn 17:26.
[336] Jn 17:21.
[337] Qo 1:2.
[338] Mt 6:34.

projections of myself, illusions… To live today in You, accepting your will that You mark in history whether I like it or not. You, and not me. You. My life is You.[339] I in You, yours… My life? How I wish it were Christ! Living in Christ. You don't speak, and I must wait. Living in You. The devil insinuates that to live in You is not to live my life but to lose it. Living in You, without sinning… Knowing how to wait is knowing a lot. Growing old, hoping in You. The strength of waiting.

The devil offers me a thousand idols, illusions: China, Russia, evangelizing… so that I may leave You, just like he tempted the monks in the desert to abandon their cells. Being Christian, it's always the same: it's the today in You, it's wanting to know nothing but You, loving You, my Lord God, and accepting that You know, that You are God and not me, that You lead history, that You save, that You are the Christ. Hoping in You and not sinning. Constantly destroying in You the idols of the imagination. To dash the children of Babylon against the rock,[340] the exaltation of self. Accepting to live in the will of another is to have encountered another, is to live in the love of God. It's to awake from Don Quixote's madness. It's living today in You. My Lord God, help me!

---

[339] Cf. Gal 2:20.
[340] Cf. Ps 137:9.

322. Psalm
Blessed be your name, Lord.
Your Kingdom come
and the creatures sing your glory.
May they know your ways on earth,
so that the people praise You.
Give me, Lord, faith that conquers the world,[341]
so that the nations may pass to You.
Remove the veil covering your people, Israel
that the resurrection from among the dead[342]
may manifest glory to the universe.

323. *Beyond me, Lord,*
yet close by you go on in this endlessness
of quieted and crumbling lights
emitting sighs confusedly.
With the soul broken
and having swallowed the unpleasantness
of being and of not being,
You, You alone.
Press me from within!
Gather me up like spilled liquid!
That my soul may exude
the desire for You,
through the baked clay
of broken tile,
a thousand scattered pieces.
With reason wounded,

---

[341] Cf. 1 Jn 5:5.
[342] Cf. Rom 11:15.

the unpleasantness of being, already swallowed,
the soul broken
amid quieted and crumbling lights,
You go beyond me, Lord,
 and I shout to You:
Quiet me inside!
Gather me up like spilled liquid!
That my soul may exude
desire for You,
through the baked clay
of those jars,
of the tiles,
of those thousand pieces gathered up.
How many dead scattered
in the gutters
 and that stench...
Press me from within, Lord!
You alone fill my heart
when the mascara
of my vanity runs.

324. I feel my spirit scattered throughout my members.
Collected in my brain, the heart is its center.
When my spirit suffers,
I give it the voice of God for nourishment...
and it is nourished or never happy.
When it quiets and calms down
it allows itself to be carried by the body,
that always roars like a bull in heat,
the desire for pleasure,
for wellbeing,

to love and be loved...
The body has its feelings and its meaning.
And I, who am I?
Body, spirit and I.
We are three, three who walk.
I decide.
Body? Spirit?
And why not the happiness of both,
which is that of all three?
And the soul?
Body, spirit, and soul.
It's the spirit of Christ
that bears witness to my spirit.[343]
And in this meeting, I follow it,
and my body, surprised,
quiets down and obeys.
My soul full of light
from the faith that illuminates my reason
and I go.

325. *Alone to alone beneath the cross, Mary.*
Who could separate you from the love of God?
Anguish? Persecution? The sword?...[344]
Alone to alone, lonely Virgin,
only Mother, tower pierced-through,
column that supports the heaven of our weak faith.
Alone to alone, little, hidden, full of God.
Pray for me, for I am a sinner.

---

[343] Cf. Rom 8:16.
[344] Cf. Rom 8:35.

326. The distinctive feature of a Christian? Discernment.
Mirror of the Christian? Prayer.
The worst thing? To judge.
The greatest of all the virtues? Discretion, discernment.
Why am I afraid? Because I still love the world.
Faced with suffering: alone to alone, with Mary.
What does it mean to be humble? Not to judge.
Denying oneself produces happiness and a good mood.
The desire to fornicate is a temptation.
The desire to do good is a grace.
Life is a great good.
Death is an evil from which the Lord saves us.
God is the very essence of being, of your being, and love is to be begotten by Him, like water, that gushes and wells up to Eternal Life.[345]

327. August 2000.
Persecution is better for the health of our faith than applause.

328. To evangelize is to carry seeds.[346]

329. To flatter a Christian is to hand him over to Satan.

330. If they persecute you, they make you strong.

---

[345] Cf. Jn 4:14.
[346] Cf. Ps 126:6.

331. To be humiliated is a grace that God sends you for you to be humble, because God gives his grace to the humble.[347]

332. To be a hypocrite, secretly fornicating, is the way to Gehenna.

333. Hypocrisy is the Pharisee's leaven.[348]

334. The hypocrite is the one who doesn't tell the truth, doesn't live in the truth, and lies to himself.

335. *Along the road he passed*
and on the earth, he left
His luminous footprints.

336. July 5, 2001.
They betrayed me, I was exposed, my friends laid a trap for me… The Lord handed me over to my enemies. Ceaselessly are enemies are heaped upon me, implacable demons who never stop. I cannot sleep, I cannot pray… Through my brain pass jailers who don't let me rest. It's very easy to say that everything is a grace…
Yes, I cannot breathe.

---

[347] Cf. Jm 4:6.
[348] Cf. Lk 12:1.

"Sit down alone and in silence, place your mouth in the dust and offer your cheeks to the one who wounds you."[349]

I am certainly a sinner. I have lied, cheated. Have I done what is evil in the sight of God and men? Yes, certainly. What am I complaining about then?

My friends have betrayed me, they have exposed me. They laid a trap, and here I am. My brain full of demons, my mouth bitter, my heart dead, my stomach hurts, and my feet would like to run to save myself...

Lord Jesus! Help me to love my enemies!

337. I picked up this notebook and I write: today, July 9, 2001.

I am emerging from a trial or terrible temptation. I have experienced the pain of suffering calumny, betrayal, and lies. They have denounced me falsely, they exposed me with lies. They sentenced me, they condemned me without listening to me.

The Lord handed me over to my enemies.

May my only glory be to resemble You, my Lord God, You crucified... You who bring Judas with you who tells lies about You, while he smiles at you and remains silent.

Strangely, when I complain and shout because of how these wounds hurt, the one who hears me smiles triumphantly and throws salt on them.

I do not know how to love my enemy.

---

[349] Cf. Lam 3:28-30.

I do not know how to suffer in silence.
I do not know how to live like a Christian.
I do not know if I have faith.

338. The keys to art, the keys to beauty... To the art of being. Beauty situates the being of that which is beautified, of that made beautiful by someone who shows through beauty that he wants to provoke pleasure in us, that he loves us. Beauty, pleasure, aesthetic emotion, joy, balance, someone behind it... Why does something seem beautiful to us? We like it, it produces a small or great pleasure in us. Pleasure?

Light, illuminating any object, exalts it, gives it its being, tells it that it exists. And nevertheless, it lives alongside other beings, which in their turn, illuminated, live without confusion. The shadows limit, separate them, enhance and situate them, producing beauty.

Life and aesthetics. Life and beauty. A painting is beautiful when it reproduces this balance of the being of things that are without confusion, in contrast and in a balance of communion and harmony, in short, of love, so to speak.

Art and beauty appear in the measure in which this is affirmed: life created, the creator. In a landscape, a tree, beautiful in itself, majestic, in the chiaroscuro of its green, compact foliage... The smooth sky enhances the beauty of the movement of the lush leaves. But the ground that sustains it also wants to be, and no less so. Each thing... its being perfect in beauty and distinction, one beside the other. Likewise, the colors, the shapes: the forehead of a face is encircled by the hair that crowns it; the eyes drawn like jewels, supported by the cheekbones, which, like faint hills of chiaroscuro, sing of the beauty of the nose and the mouth... The sharpness, the smoothness of a surface, the hardness of a line... everything always supported by its opposite, which enhances it, saying: let us help each other to be. "Everything exalts the beauty of the other."[350]

And, in the measure that we are, love appears, art appears, aesthetic emotion, when things are in the love of the balance of communion, of the being of things, of the beings of life...

Life moves us when it appears over death. God is he who is.[351] God is in things and it moves us that they exist. Yes, they are, we are. Yes, we are, we live. And why? We have been sketched, loved and placed in life. We are alongside others, but we are and that is enough. We are alongside emotionless things. We are in light and in time. We are. Are we or do we exist? To exist and to be. We exist because we have been put here in order to love.

339. "Love and do what you will."[352]

This articulates the relationship of things among themselves. It is the dialogue of love where the

---

[350] Cf. Sir 42:25.
[351] Cf. Ex 3:14.
[352] Cf. St. Augustine, *on First Letter of John* 7,8

related communicate themselves in a complex way... The other is the important one. And beauty awakens like a light appearing in the relationship. "Each thing enhances the beauty of the other."[353]

And what is the relationship of the most perfect in love? How much green enhances and illuminates red the most? Which rocky material is enhanced by the green of the moss that covers it?

The smooth hills of cheekbones enhance the fine drawing of the eyes, like jewels, the forehead, the hair... Beauty in the perfect proportion of love, the smoothness of the blue sky sings of the beauty of the capricious clouds. In everything we see, there is art. The blurring of the shadows sings of the outlines... In itself, everything is a language of relationship. And history? What is its relationship? The events come and sing of a duty that is related to the event, a relationship of love with Him who put us into history...

340. A *midrash* says:

"'When will the Messiah come?'

'Today.'

'And where is he?'

'Among the lepers begging for alms.'

'And how can one recognize him?'

'He is the one adjusting his bandages to be able to come at once.'"[354]

---

[353] Cf. Sir 42:25.
[354] Cf. *Talmud, Sanhedrin* 98a.

Among the poor, he is ready to depart. The Messiah comes, departs to save and goes with you. In the shantytown of Palomeras, in the Borghetto Latino of Rome, in the Fosso di Sant'Agnese, also in Rome, in A Curraleira in Lisbon. Among the poor, adjusting his bandages, to be ready. When will the Messiah come? Today.

341. Adjusting the bandages, one by one, the bandages covering the wounds of our sins. Wrapped in bandages and in a manger lies a newborn child. That will be the sign.[355]

"Peter rose and ran to the sepulcher. He bent down, but only saw the burial cloths..."[356] And John "stooping to look in, he saw the linen cloths lying there, but he did not go in. Then Simon Peter came, following him, and went into the tomb. He saw the linen cloths lying there, as well as the cloth that had been wrapped around Jesus' head, not with the burial cloths but rolled up in a separate place."[357]

"Lazarus, come out!" And the dead came out, tied hand and foot with bandages and face wrapped in a shroud. Jesus tells them, "Unbind him and let him go."[358]

---

[355] Cf. Lk 2:12.

[356] Cf. Lk 24:12.

[357] Jn 20:5-7. In the Spanish bible, what the English translates as "linen cloths" (and "burial cloths" in the preceding passage) is translated as *vendas*, "bandages".

[358] Cf. Jn 11:43-44.

The bandages on the ground are no longer necessary. Christ is risen! Our body has been cured. The shroud that covered the face of death is folded in a separate place.

And St. Paul says that Christ died for all, therefore all have died; "and he died so that those who live no longer live for themselves..."[359] This death is offered freely. This oblation, this sacrifice, is given to you so that you may live forever, so that you may give yourself.

Leprosy for him; for you, healing. He doesn't live for himself, but for you. This love, this energy, called *CARITAS*, permeates the universe. It is his glory. "*Deus caritas est.*"[360] God is, in Christ crucified, total gift... And he descended into Hell.

And I suffer at the thought that I don't know how to say it or announce it, if they don't believe me. I will adjust the bandages and be ready. Among the poor, I will wait to go out... Today. When will the Messiah come? Today. "If today you listen to his voice, do not harden your heart."[361] I am a sinner. He is the Messiah, and He calls me so that I may take up the bandages and go among the lepers to be credible and to save.

342. I return to this notebook today, September 24, 2001.

---

[359] Cf. 2 Cor 5:14-15.
[360] 1 Jn 4:8,16.
[361] Cf. Ps 95:7-8.

After unspeakable sufferings, You have had mercy and have helped us. Three new *Redemptoris Mater* seminaries were born: Sydney, in Australia, Washington, in the United States, and Goma, in Congo, Africa.

Maybe a war will erupt: terrorists, the terrible act of the Twin Towers in New York, the apostasy of Europe... And you, Lord, my God, the sweetest, best and most holy in the world.

You made me cry when I went to embrace my enemy and that surprised me. I hadn't cried for a long time. I said to him, "Forgive me, I am sorry for having made you suffer." And suddenly a profound sobbing took over my body. He embraced me and didn't know what to do, while I cried...

343. I've gone through a really difficult time. It's what I deserved. And if I abandon You, I will experience worse. In any case, I learned three things: 1st, my little faith, for I don't know how to love my enemy; 2nd, that I have had to pray in order not to die, and this helped me; 3rd, that I saw the devil: he didn't scare me very much; it was a warning because I can be condemned and fall into the hands of the one who is nothing. I hope to be faithful. The first two Neocatechumenal communities in China were born. They told us that in the convivence at the end of the catechesis, one of the co-responsibles recounted the reason he had gone to listen to the catechesis although he was not from the parish nor

from that town. He said that his 30-year-old son told him the Virgin Mary had appeared to him in dreams, along with his wife who had died two years prior, accompanied by two angels, and that she had told him, "Go and tell your father to go to such and such town 40 kilometers away because two foreign missionaries have arrived, and that he should go to the catechesis." He set out and arrived on Monday when the catechesis began. In the end, a community of 72 brothers and sisters was born.

344. To separate oneself from everything to be alone with Christ brings the desire for self-mortification. Mortification for Christ brings us to tears. Tears, to holy fear. Fear produces humility. Holy humility leads us to spiritual vision, and this precedes and leads us to charity, to divine love in us, which makes us free of emotion and close to God.

345. The Desert Fathers said, "Keep an unkempt look, your garment dirty, your clothing poor, your customs should be simple, your words sincere, no haughty gait, your voice without affectation, live in poverty, allow yourself to be despised by everyone, your mind always on the Lord, sober and constant in suffering discomforts for Christ."
Fight against the devil, who wants to dirty your soul, and live without a city, without a home, without anything that is yours, a foreigner, a pilgrim, an itinerant, be humble, compassionate, good, meek, patient, merciful, full of peace.

346. I am in Manila. We had a convivence of the itinerant catechists of Asia. It was wonderful. We are beginning. The Cardinal Prefect of the Congregation for the Evangelization of Peoples came at the end, and told us, "The Prefect and all the Congregation exist to help you to fulfill your missionary vocation.
You are missionaries of the frontier, of the frontlines. We are in the rearguard to help and support you, so that your mission may be fulfilled day by day." The families in mission spoke. They are heroic: the weather, the language, the devil, etc. Sufferings, accusations, calumnies...
Popular or natural religiosity, if it is not evangelized and catechized by a serious catechumenate, cannot hold up in the face of social change, of secularization, the sects, Islam... Our communities are persecuted in the Philippines; generally, they are ignored by the priests, who barely help them. The Lord will help us.

347. Prayer before going to bed:
Blessed are You, Lord,
who give us sleep, to rest.
May my bed be a perfect altar before You.
May I not sleep the slumber of death.
Blessed are You, Lord,
who illuminate the universe with your glory.

348. *Architrave,*
architect,

small jar,
food for birds
art…
Art of loving,
of being in You…
Conqueror
of death.
In the streets
full of cars.
It's going to rain.
It's cold,
the day is dreary.
and You…
A drunk
laying in a doorway,
among cardboard boxes.
A terrible
attack,
and to walk
toward the center
of things.
Do not take away
your tenderness.
Do not withdraw
your friendship.
Help me, Lord!
Have mercy.

349. To be successful in this life is a trap. It leads to adulation and lies… The only happiness in this life

lies not in success but in helping others, in loving, in doing good to someone.
Life was given to us to love God and mankind.
If they applaud you, they lie to you, they hand you over to Satan.
We are not satisfied in being praised, but by doing good.

350. November 24, 2001.
I return to these pages, after a long absence, with the need to speak... to unburden myself... Your Word has been transformed in my heart, in my head, in my hands, into a fire that scorches and burns... "Love your enemies."

"Do not resist evil... If someone takes what is yours, do not claim it back..."[362] Lord Jesus, your words burn me, incinerate within me everything that is not Christian. The Hebrew letters are like flames that your finger inscribed on the stone.[363] Tongues of fire in the heart, on the head...[364] "Love as I have loved you."[365]

I am not Christian; I am a sinner. Your nature within me, where is it? What remains of my Baptism? Put within me a new spirit, "a steadfast spirit."[366] Give me your Spirit.

---

[362] Cf. Mt 5:39,44; Lk 6:30.
[363] Cf. Ex 31:18.
[364] Cf. Ac 2:3.
[365] Cf. Jn 13:34.
[366] Cf. Ps 51:10.

"Love your enemies."³⁶⁷ The enemy detests you, hates you; if you die, it's a relief for him...
Your Word does not allow me to live; morning, noon, and night it burns my insides,³⁶⁸ burning in my soul like the burning bush.³⁶⁹ Your Word, your Word, the thorns of the bush, the fire. And You, Lord, my God.

351. Living among enemies. Living in an environment that tramples and detests your commandments. "All are corrupted, they do abominable things... "³⁷⁰ Evil, good, your Word, my sins and death... Only the tenderness of your love that I no longer feel, in this night, in the gloom of this dark faith... Lord, help me!
"Courage, for I will help you!" You respond within me.

352. "If God, being able to help, doesn't help, he is a monster, and if he cannot help, it means He is not God," says Nietzsche... and how can we respond? How far can you help? Until death: one can do no more... God helped us that far, to the point of death, for Christ crucified is God. And why are things like this? Because we know nothing of God, nor of love, nor of freedom... Only that which He

---

³⁶⁷ Mt 5:44.
³⁶⁸ Cf. Rev. 10:9-10.
³⁶⁹ Cf. Ex 3:2.
³⁷⁰ Cf. Ps 53:1-3.

Himself revealed to us in Christ,[371] radiance of glory and imprint of the substance of God.[372]

353. *There is a love that makes the heart hurt,*
there is a pain that is full of love…
It is absence.
And in this evil of absence
there is a humility that makes us cry
for not having loved more, and now…
it's irreparable, no longer there.
He left without our love
and it is painful that he left without our love...
I exist to love and I have not loved:
I go, without fulfilment,
I go toward the emptiness of my works.
There is a love that makes the heart hurt…
Why does it hurt us not to have loved?
What is love?
We are in the absolute You.
We are in the desert embracing You, Lord,
and in You, everyone, into infinity.
Absence of God.
If God is lacking,
what pain, what poverty,
what humility, what abandonment.
It's your little son lying in the street, alone and dead,
and your Mother's heart…
aching with love.

---

[371] Cf. Mt 11:27.
[372] Cf. Heb 1:3.

354. *I pull away from You, and I don't want to,*
and I pull away... and I don't want to...
and I pull away.
Take pity...
Lord, take pity.
Return, make me return to You.

355. *The abandonment of the poor*
in that orphanage full of rats,
smelling of urine.
Those children... some mentally handicapped.
I am not against anyone or against God.
I am grateful to these children,
to these poor ones,
who bring me close to the mystery of my own being.
Only one answer:
outside the city, bloodied,
You, Lord, my God,
crucified and dead for me...

356. There is no greater grace today than to live the faith in a Christian community: it is the Body of the risen Christ.

357. The community is a school of love for the other. Humility, simplicity, and praise, a way that brings us to discover that the other is Christ. Community like the Holy, like the Sacred Family of Nazareth.[373]

---

[373] Cf. supra, footnote 234.

358. The community that meets in the home of Rafa or of Giampiero is an *ecclesia*, is a body. Is it the temple of God on earth? Is it the body of Christ? Am I a member of the body of Christ? My life is part of a new liturgy whose new form of worship is evangelization;[374] in history, in my daily history, a liturgy of holiness whose ritual is the psalter; in the psalms it is written of me and of life...

"Rabbi, eat." "I have a food to eat that you do not know about... My food is to do the will of the One who has sent me and to accomplish his *work*."[375] The work of God... "Father, may none of those you have given me be lost, may I *raise* them on the last day."[376]

"Look, the fields are ripe for the harvest... I send you to reap what you have not sown. So that in you, the saying may be fulfilled, 'some labor and suffer in sowing, and others profit and harvest what they have not worked for...' Well, I send you to collect the fruit of what others have sown, and you will profit from their efforts."[377]

Labor of Christ. He sowed his blood in the furrow of history and the life of man. The fields are already ready for the harvest of the nations. Spiritual worship, liturgy of holiness, St. Paul calls the evangelization.[378] To turn our hearts to God is a

---

[374] Cf. Rom 1:9; 15:16.
[375] Cf. Jn 4:31-34.
[376] Cf. Jn 6:39-40.
[377] Cf. Jn 4:35-37.
[378] Cf. Rom 1:9; 15:16.

new oblation. In the ancient sacrifices the gods were offered the heart of animal victims, sheep, cows… We offer a more perfect worship in Christ, who gave his blood for mankind. We offer, through the evangelization of the itinerants, hearts that convert to God and love. Upon the altar of the cross of daily history, we offer our hearts to God, to his will. Only in his will lies global salvation. "For your sake, Lord, we are sheep brought to the slaughter every day."[379] "And he stretched out his arms on the cross *and gained for You a holy people.*"[380]

359. January 2, 2002.
Love for You, Lord, my God,
is like a sea of purest sapphire.
The light, your light,
illuminates the depth of my deepest being
and calls me.
There is no light equal to another.
Your light is from paradise:
The feeling of perfect joy at your right hand…

360. Convert today and the world will be redeemed!

361. *The air has become heavy.*
The feeling of your love
has closed the window.
My soul is hidden…

---

[379] Cf. Ps 44:11,22; Rom 8:36.
[380] Cf. *Eucharistic Prayer II.*

and in the bottom of my cup
Are the dregs of anguish.
"What can I do if I lack hope,
the hope that comes from the Lord?
Sit down alone and in silence,
because the Lord has laid it upon you,
put your mouth in the dust,
there may yet be hope.
Offer your cheek to him who strikes you...
because the Lord does not cast off forever;
even if he afflicts you, he will then be merciful..."[381]

I feel that I will be condemned. I am a sinner, ungrateful, one who places burdens, who doesn't fulfill, nor move, not even my little finger.[382] A hypocrite, a Pharisee, as Carmen calls me. One who says but doesn't do.[383]

I lack your friendship, Lord Jesus,
You are angry with me, take pity.
Without your love, what is life?
For without You, Lord, I do not want to live.

362.   *The deepest part of my personal being...*
       an intense blue,
       a floor of purest sapphire...
       Am I an unfinished being?

---

[381] Cf. Lam 3:18,28-32.
[382] Cf. Mt 23:4.
[383] Cf. Mt 23:3.

Am I an evolution?
Do I lack a woman...?
What am I?
One who walks.
My being is the walking,
My deepest being, walking.
Toward what?
Toward where?
Walking for the sake of it?
No!
Walking toward You.
Do I search and move
toward a total fullness of love
that encompasses everyone within it?

363. If everything is going well, it's not going well.

364. "One day Rabbi Joshua ben Levi asked the prophet Elijah, "When will the Messiah come?" Elijah responded, "Go and ask him." Rabbi Joshua said, "And where is he?" And Elijah, "On the outskirts of the city of Rome." "And how will I recognize him?" "He lives among the lepers who beg for alms." "And how will I recognize him?" "While all the lepers, when they arrive, remove the bandages that cover their diseased skin, the Messiah takes them off one by one and then puts them on again. He thinks that God could call him at any moment to bring redemption, and he is always ready." Rabbi Joshua went to look for him and greeted him, "Peace be with you, teacher." "Peace be with you,

son of Levi." "When will you come, teacher?" "Today." Later, Rabbi Joshua ben Levi complained to Elijah, "The Messiah lied to me. He said that he would come today, and he hasn't come." And Elijah told him, "You did not understand him well. He cited Psalm 95:7, which says, 'Today, if you hear his voice...!'"[384]

This Hebrew *midrash* reminded me of the shantytown in Palomeras, where the Lord brought me. And the shantytowns of Rome, where I went to wait for the Lord to call me. After visiting some pastors, accompanied by Fr. Dino Torreggiani, and having seen they weren't welcome me, nor needed any way of conversion in their parishes, I decided to go to the outskirts of the city to live with the poor and there wait for the Lord to open a way, and so it happened.

There is a "today" open to receive the Messiah, who through us comes to the world to bring redemption. Convert today, and the world will be redeemed! "If you listen to his voice..."[385]

The voice of God, his Word, is Christ. In Him is the fullness of divinity.[386] He is fullness of love toward man in world history. He is the Alpha and the Omega.[387] In Him I can participate in cosmic, historical, complete salvation.

---

[384] Cf. *Talmud, Sanhedrin* 98a.
[385] Cf. Ps 95:7.
[386] Cf. Col 2:9.
[387] Cf. Rev. 1:8.

The thirst for love, the suffering of living in a world contrary to the Gospel... "If today you listen to his voice..."[388] "His voice." His will is Christ, who was crucified for me. The love that God, in Christ, has for me has made me a new creature, a new person, a child of God. His nature rescues me from death.

365. "The Lord helped me."[389] This is my constant experience facing so many difficulties and anguishes. Fear, tiredness, insults, shouts... "The Lord helped me."
Before me is the convivence of Asian Bishops in Malaysia. I have no strength... The Lord will help me!

366. April 9, 2002.
We had the convivence of Asian bishops in Kota Kinabalu, on the island of Java. 120 bishops came: 50 from India, 26 from the Philippines, and others from Vietnam, Laos, Japan, and also from Australia, Oceania, etc. As always, the Lord helped us. A passing of the Lord in a great communion, in the surprise of all that they heard and in that the Lord made them experience. A true "Pentecost."
From there, we left for China, to Beijing. Then to Japan and to the island of Taiwan. The Lord went before us with his Spirit and accompanied us in every moment. The meetings on the island of

---

[388] Cf. Ps 95:7.
[389] Cf. Ps 118:13.

Taiwan, with the presence of Cardinal Shan de Kaohsiung, were wonderful. Soon, in this last diocese, we will begin construction of the new building of the *Redemptoris Mater* Seminary.

367. Death and resurrection. Anguish and thanksgiving because the Lord helped me. I live constantly in a task that is beyond me: fear and joy, anguish and consolation... How good the Lord is! Holy, holy, holy. The Lord always helps us. His love and my constant infidelity touch me. His Word is constantly fulfilled: "I sent you to reap what you did not sow. Others labored, and you profit from their labor."[390] Christ labored and suffered sowing his blood for the salvation of every man. He sent us to harvest in joy, *so that He may rejoice* with us in the moment of the harvest, gathering the sheaves.[391]

368. In Russia, in that orphanage of abandoned children... You, my God. Children, mentally challenged, that sour smell... To escape, to leave, to where?

Those lonely elderly people, constantly turning their heads toward the door, hoping to see a relative arrive. Mechanical gestures that remind me of that bear in the zoo in a narrow cage, who crazily repeated the same head movements over and over. Old people alone, alone and elderly. Are they

---

[390] Cf. Jn 4:38.
[391] Cf. Jn 4:36; Ps 126:6.

people? Things tossed aside. And You, my Lord God, are there. I will go in and kneel among the old people, among the children of that orphanage…

Places of loneliness. Only your presence in the desert of death. The children, the old people, have your grace: *innocence that touches my soul*. Like that man condemned to death…. Alone among the guards, they take him to be killed; innocence, loneliness, he's the last one on earth: they take him to be killed. And those sick with AIDS, skinny as greyhounds and alone, go to die hopelessly.

Humility and innocence, loneliness that only You fill. Oh! If you didn't exist, what pain. And they brought you to die, roped to other prisoners. And your blood stained the street and there your blood remained, my Jesus.

369. We went up to the television tower. We were in China, Beijing. We extended our hands and, pointing at the devil, we demanded of him, in the name of our Lord, Jesus of Nazareth, to abandon Beijing, China, and to go to the Gobi Desert…

Afterward, from that tower, we called the Holy Spirit: Come, Holy Spirit…! And suddenly a white dove appeared that fluttered around us. We applauded it and it left and returned three times. It was a good omen, a sign. We were very high up, about 400 meters.

After, we had wonderful meetings and there the bandages and shroud remained,[392] and He, risen, goes ahead of us to Galilee, on the other side of the sea, Galilee of the gentiles:[393] China.

370. Why are you crying, my soul? Do not be afraid. "Give me your sins, I will take them," the Lord tells me. "It's my being, the deepest part, loving you, certainly loving you like this." O Lord! How can I give you my sins? They fill you with death. Oh, holy humility of Christ, who could find you!

371. To bear injuries, insults, shouting; that everything falls apart around You; my desert will be where You and I are alone. Totally with You, saving, being with You, being one. Oh, holy humility of Christ, who could find you!

372. For without You, Lord, I do not want life. You withdrew your friendship from me, the light went out, everything around me is dark, without any beauty; without your love, what pain, what loneliness, what hell... Lord, take pity! Return! Return!

373. June 29, 2002, Feast of St. Peter and St. Paul.
The Holy See has approved the *Statutes* of the Way as a Christian initiation, as a post-baptismal

---

[392] Cf. Jn 20:6-7.
[393] Cf. Mt 28:7; 4:15.

Catechumenate... Blessed be the Lord! I deserve nothing, only that my sins be uncovered... and the truth be seen: that I am worth nothing. Lord, have mercy, for I have no strength left!

374. Sillian (Austria), July 18, 2002.
I wandered slowly through life
and I stood with mouth agape, upon realizing
that I was capable of doing evil
and that I was doing it.
I encountered you
and stopped in surprise.
I fell into a ravine
and heard a braying[394]
as the blind sun awakened me.
In the desert...
Your body,
such a beautiful flower...
that my heart could not cut...
Because You have grasped my soul
with your hands
and my life is going away.

I will repay you everything, wait.[395] Do not correct me in your anger, in your wrath, do not punish me...[396] Have mercy!

---

[394] The mosaics of Aquileia depict a donkey braying, representing the devil who 'brays' on hearing the *kerygma*.
[395] Cf. Mt 18:26.
[396] Cf. Ps 6:1.

375. 25th of September, in this walk, in the year two thousand and two.
Sixty-three years
And I go…
Oh, who could walk with you!
The absolute of being.
In you, sated, in my deepest being.
The absolute of my being
is to love everything in You:
in the praise of your glory,
for you are, my Lord God.

376. The Desert Fathers say, "Woe to the man whose fame surpasses his works!" The devil has launched against me flattery, fame, newspapers… above all in Spain. In Italy, calumnies, denounced for heresy, lies… Carmen crucified with a depression that makes her feel dead: her faith edifies me… Mario cannot take it anymore, with his extremely weak health, everything with great fatigue. And I… a sinner. I seem to have lost the friendship of God. And He's right, because I am not faithful. May reproach and slander befall me.
And what can I do? "Sit down alone and in silence, offer your cheek to the one who strikes you… Place your mouth in the dust…"[397] Embrace the cross and hope in the Lord.
I am incapable without feeling You, Lord, my God. Have mercy! Have mercy! They hate me, they want

---

[397] Cf. Lam 3:28-30.

to kill me. Have mercy! They cannot bear the approval of the *Statutes*. Furious, they spout blasphemies, even against the Church that has approved us.

The Pope received us in Castel Gandolfo. All the itinerants, the pastors and responsibles of the oldest communities were there with us. When we went to greet him, he gave Carmen and me a kiss, demonstrating in front of everyone the love he has for us. Lord, give the Pope health, prophetic strength, and consolation!

377. Today, October 4, 2002, Feast of St. Francis of Assisi.

What can I say about St. Francis? That Christ looked at him and his life changed. Your glance, Lord, is the grace that transforms us and enamors us, that makes us follow you... It's your glance that makes us see you in everything... You, my Jesus and my God. It is the history that you construct with us, a way that sings of your love and our weakness, your mercy and our infidelity, your tenderness and our laziness, indifference, selfishness, lust... powerlessness, sickness, weariness... And You who do not judge us, who help us, who wait for us, who forgive us, who always forgive us.

Faith by itself, without feelings, can penetrate the veil and part the curtains of heaven and its brilliant light... It's the image that all around us, in its harmony and beauty, shows that You love us. Beauty is a mirror of love.

378. The beauty of all that surrounds us in nature is a mirror of the love that God has for mankind. The light, the weather… The unpredictable is beauty of love, movement… Everything is threatened in love. Being and death, the light and beauty; the animals look at us, and there they are there, impassive, speaking to us of You.
And evil? Lies, deceit. Hatred… and they were killing each other. Stealing, lying, cheating, making money. Money… so many times it suffocates the soul. *"Misterium iniquitatis."*[398]
There the devil is, against Christ, against the Church, against you, against me, against everyone.
Yesterday, on television they said that somewhere in the world a person commits suicide every 60 seconds. They are killing themselves, continually, and they don't know that You, my Lord God, have conquered death. Light, time, death… Heaven and You, who love us.
Free, to be free from money, from health, from the body, from vices and lusts, from affections… Free! Freed by You, free with You. One's being recollected with You. One with You and everyone in You.

---

[398] 2 Thes 2:7.

379. November 28, 2002.
I would like to vent. I am caught in a trap. I am submerged in a temptation that doesn't let me breathe, doesn't let me sleep... What pain! The Lord is silent. I have the feeling that I will not be able to resist, that I will go crazy. My mind goes round and round unceasingly. I cannot pray. My God, have mercy!

380. Lord Jesus, my God, have mercy! I find myself in total weakness. Do not abandon me, Lord. Virgin Mary, intercede for me. Everything is my fault, it's my sins... Help me, Lord! Help me for I am without strength.

*"How do you endure O life,
not living where you live,
and being brought near death
by the arrows you receive
from that which you conceive of your Beloved?"*[399]

381. *I would like to be
crying
of your infinite love
the pauper,
the besieged,
wounded heart,
who from that cliff
beholds the raging sea.*

---

[399] St. John of the Cross, *Spiritual Canticle*.

> *The soul roars*
> *with the bellow of*
> *that hunted stag,*
> *of wounded heart.*
> *And I*
> *would like to be, crying…*
> *of your ravished,*
> *wounded love,*
> *heart,*
> *of the soul, the stag.*
> *The sea…*
> *of your infinite love.*

382. July 7, 2003.

    I am in Sillian. I arrived yesterday. I hope to rest, but without you, I cannot.

383. You know, Lord, the temptation and test in which I find myself. You know my surprise at seeing that I am capable of doing the evil that I do not want to do.[400] So many times, you helped me… with You at my right hand, I will not waver.[401]

384. > *The weeds grow*
    > *in my garden*
    > *and the pain that*
    > *it produces in me….*
    > *It destroys the wheat*

---

[400] Cf. Rom 7:19.
[401] Cf. Ps 16:8.

*of my compassionate
love
and I must
accept it.
They are my sins
that surprise me.
Lord, have mercy!*

385. *It is in the puddles
of that putrefaction
that the
black boar
wallows.
It's the surprise
of that indifference.
Do not withdraw
your friendship from me,
Jesus, my God,
for I will die.
And contemplating the
indifference of things
and the time
that watches me
and I would like to live
permeated by time
by things and by You.
Have mercy.*

386. Today, Thursday, June 3, 2004.
I return to these pages after having been rattled and shaken, exposed to public derision, insulted…

They called me to paint in the cathedral of Madrid, an honor I do not deserve. In the apse of the cathedral, I painted a large Pantocrator that presides over the whole transept. There are seven large panels like a *Crown of Mysteries*: the Baptism of the Lord, the Transfiguration, the Crucifixion, the Pantocrator, the Resurrection, the Ascension, and Pentecost. Above the paintings, 7 stained glass windows and, below the Pantocrator, a large stained-glass window depicting the risen Christ.

In the cathedral Prince Felipe and Princess Letizia were married. The wedding was televised, and they say that it was seen throughout the world: 1.2 billion people. The paintings in the apse were seen very little because a campaign had already been unleashed against me and the paintings.

After the wedding, a surprising persecution was unleashed. Insulting articles began to appear in the newspapers: "Sanctimonious dauber has filled the cathedral with smears," for example. Every day criticisms appeared about the ugliness of the cathedral and, above all, the *Crown of Mysteries*. The first accusation that hurt me very much was that I was a beginner and not a professional, accusing Cardinal Rouco most of all. The second was that the paintings were a plagiarism of a painter from Santo Domingo, of the Chapel of the *Redemptoris Mater* Seminary. I commissioned those paintings, copies of the *Crown of Mysteries* I painted in Florence. The worst thing is that the accusation of plagiarism was broadcast on all the news. The storm continued, as prominent personages, such as the writers Antonio Gala and Francisco Umbral, added their signatures... The climax came when the television news said that the Royal Academy of Fine Arts had issued a statement condemning the paintings for their poor quality, etc.

One linguist wrote an article comparing me to a pesky bedbug that needs to be exterminated. He concludes: "But there are bedbugs against which one must employ a great number of exterminators, which still would not be enough. Who dares now to fight against this enormous and terrible bedbug, who shouts his triumph at night beneath the sputtering of candles that rule malignantly in the [Cathedral of the] Almudena, and celebrates black masses in honor of this triumphant trickery, almost as in a horror scene?"

387. Sillian, July 2004.
It is your friendship, Lord,
that I desire.
It is your friendship felt.
It is your love...
And in the depths of my soul
a dark and black hole
that prevents me from feeling your presence.
Forgive me, Lord,
forgive me...
You gave me, you have given me,
a soul to accompany me,
so that I may seek You,

to embrace you,
to love you,
to encounter you,
and today I feel it broken
and it doesn't receive your love,
and I am alone,
How horrible...
My soul feels downcast, Oh!
From the depths of my being,
the deepest part.
Not even your love is felt, what pain!
My being and You
in my soul they meet and love one another,
but my soul broke and I don't feel You.
A black hole
and the feeling of your presence escapes me.
And your friendship and things harden
and time rises to accuse me...
But You reestablish me,
You have stitched up my soul.
Yes, You love me!
You have forgiven my sins!
To live, to be in You!

388. *And I go*
toward the nothingness of my works...
The water runs
under that open faucet
and runs...
As my life goes...
As my life runs

> *toward nothingness…*
> *Where are you,*
> *Oh, holy humility of Christ?*
> *I am here,*
> *standing in front of the door of death.*

389. August 18, 2004.
> *Do I have the fear of the Lord?*
> *Do I speak with God without ceasing?*
> *Do I hope in God?*
> *To fear always.*
> *To pray always.*
> *To hope always.*
> *Woe is me,*
> *for I love sin more than I love You!*
> *Jesus, my God, have mercy.*
> *My life without You,*
> *without your friendship,*
> *how difficult…*
> *Have mercy!*

390. Why must I bear all mankind in my heart? You have expanded my heart. I suffer for Spain, for Africa, for Russia… for the youth, the families, the elderly… for mankind. I will go out and show my wounded heart, hurt by your love for mankind. Blood and water,[402] immense compassion, your cross, a banner of sufferings.

---

[402] Cf. Jn 19:34.

Oh, who would be able to sail with you, love with you, so deeply as to lose myself in forgetfulness of self! I saw You and I found You and in You I was able to embrace those who are my own, forever.

391. You have given me your heart, and I feel blood and water running. The blood of your love for all mankind, the water of the evangelization, the Baptism in your cross with which you killed death and crucified sin.

392. How many times have I returned to You, wounded from so many battles, and what a great ovation by the angels upon seeing me... Like when the victorious army entered and the people, overjoyed, thronged together to receive them; what a great ovation when the wounded were paraded. No injured man is a dishonor for the nation upon return from battle; only the deserters who go over to the enemy. That is what the Fathers of the Church said. How much pain my sins have caused in my soul. Without You, Lord, Hell. Oh, my Jesus, have mercy!

393. The year 2004 comes to an end and the water flows, carrying so many branches and hundreds of thousands of cadavers in Asia... My life is passing, and I am always worse. I live off You and your love, and, if you are lacking, what pain...

394. *In time, and with time, I go*
and things gaze at me

silently, quietly,
and I go toward You... Oh!
in this being toward You.
What pain.
Come! Descended from the cross
and in the arms of your little Mother,
I feel my heart pacified
from the groaning of my sins.
Woe is me!
I would like to be, crying...
the embraced friend, You, my God.

395. I'm about to turn 66 and the crow of my many sins caws high on the eaves. I am incapable of restraint, and my life crumbles like bread that has hardened over time. Only You sustain me in this walk toward death. The thought of You, who are infinitely merciful. And I... The days shorten. Time presses and each day shortens more quickly.

    Woe to the man whose fame exceeds his works! Woe to the wretch that I am!

    Who can heal me?
    The quieting of things.
    And contemplating their indifference.
    In my own reflection... You.
    Laying in a doorway among cardboard boxes,
    in an odor of misery and sour urine,
    a man defeated and dejected,
    a poor man cringing and coiled
    like a snail among the cabbages.

It is man reflected in his nothingness,
in the indifference of so many...
And his children moved out
and his wife left,
Yes, she left with another man.
Oh, indifference!
Oh, infirmities!
And in my own reflection
my sins burden me.
Lord, help me!
Forgive me!
May your Spirit of love seal me
and arm the reflection of myself within me.
Why did they go to live among cardboard boxes?
My God, your love...

396. I am in Paris, February 24, 2005.
It has snowed... From the depths of my being, the deepest part, I need You, I call You, Friend, come! Jesus, my God, for I die. The beauty of being that You give us: "You are my son, today I have begotten you."[403]

397. I set this song dedicated to the Holy Virgin Mary to music. I am in Paris. I will teach it in the Easter announcement to be sung on Good Friday. Help me, Lord. Enlighten me about what I should do with the first community of Paris. With Carmen, it's difficult. Mario's health is worse and worse. And

---

[403] Cf. Ps 2:7; Heb 5:5.

I... in You, everything. I would like to be *all yours*, my Jesus. You love me so much it makes me ashamed.

Lone to alone
under the cross,
Mary, who could separate you?
Lonely Virgin, Mother
pierced-through tower.
pillar of love,
You uphold the heaven
of our little faith.
Lone to alone,
Mother, full of God.
Pray for us
for we are sinners.
Lone to alone *under the cross.*

398. Everything exists because it is loved. In him we live, we move, we exist.[404] In Him who is love. In loving us, He gives us being. I would like to touch the depth of my personal being in order to give it, and, in giving myself, be in You and in everything.

399. I return to these pages, and I'm still alive. The Synod on the Eucharist in which I participated as an "auditor" has ended. The Congregation for Worship is examining our liturgy. The Lord will help us. Little by little, I am being left with nothing, less Christian... Maybe God wants me to consider

---

[404] Cf. Ac 17:28.

myself the last one and the worst of all. To everyone I say: pray for me, so that I don't go to Hell. Bearing with patience my own unworthiness. I am a sinner.

400. What is humility? It is considering oneself a sinner. Interior silence is a work of humility, which means not judging anyone, considering oneself worse than everyone else. Oh, holy humility of Christ, who could find you!

401. "Yes, it's enough to humble oneself and bear sweetly one's own imperfection; therein lies true holiness," says St. Teresa of the Child Jesus.[405] Accepting love as the earth accepts the rain. Jesus loves us truly, totally, to the end… Accepting the degree to which we are sinners; "bearing sweetly one's own imperfection…" The veil of heaven is removed and the purest light, crystal clear and sharp, of the love of God for us… Without judging? From the cross? We are lost sheep, full of beatings, full of wounds. Disbelieving any love. Oh, holy humility of Christ… who could find you!

402. *My days grow shorter*
and I am being left with nothing.
I would like to tell You that I love You.
The beauty of things
and the whisper of You
in the days of my life…

---

[405] Cf. *Letters of St. Teresa of the Child Jesus to her sister Celine*, n. 348.

403. *If you feel love,*
you feel it for everyone.
And He descended into Hell.
The immensity of the universe,
the endlessness of being,
the light that leaves us...
Only the weakness of God is so strong...[406]
Christ made himself sin.[407]
Who will believe it,
even if we announce it?
Who will give credence to our announcement?[408]
It is a work so great, so strong...
The weakness of God...
He no longer speaks.
His silence before evil,
before pain, before terrible violence.
He is crucified for all.
He descended into Hell.
Dark caves,
full of gaunt faces.
And in that home for the elderly,
in that residence,
a man alone,
in a wheelchair,
doesn't speak,
hasn't spoken for three years.
When he became an invalid
his wife abandoned him.

---

[406] Cf. 1 Cor 1:25.
[407] Cf. 2 Cor 5:21.
[408] Cf. Rom 10:16.

His three children put him there
and in these three years
never came to see him.
Alone, faced with himself.
Alone before death.
A brother of the Way,
family in mission,
works there
cleaning restrooms and floors
and observes him.
He pushes the wheelchair without wanting to,
speaks to him, wants to console him,
his heart aches
seeing the loneliness of being abandoned.
Oh, who could console,
love everyone with your love,
with your Spirit!
So many lonely people,
abandoned by others.
So many drink and kill themselves.
And in this loneliness full of howls... You,
little, little,
You made yourself sin for us,
descended into Hell
and broke the chains,
opened the doors,
the light entered
and we saw those black faces
of sunken and shiny eyes,
of frightened gaze,
that made one want to cry on seeing them...

It is Auschwitz.
The dark prisons of a hundred nations.
The thousands upon thousands of broken marriages,
full of hatred and insults,
that wound and beat their children
who, astonished, see how their parents
hate and insult each other:
something breaks inside forever.
I said inside.
And who could enter in that destroyed inside,
in that place of their being, the deepest part,
there where beauty, innocence,
purity and love,
have been broken
shattered to pieces?
Oh! Who could heal me...?
Thanks be given to You,
Lord Jesus,
who descended into Hell.
Your spirit,
which descended from heaven to men
entering within us, cures us,
gives us again our being in You,
a hundredfold.
It is your Spirit
who gives witness to our spirit
that you exist, that you love us,
that you adopt us as your children.[409]
Recreated in Christ,

---

[409] Cf. Rom 8:16.

we are for You forever
one in You, one in all.

404. I am in Paris. March 1, 2006. Ash Wednesday.
Life is a power, an impressive force of love. God exists, and things are about to burst into light, in an explosion of untenable love. And we will all be transformed.[410]

The Pope has granted us the liturgy. Fantastic for the mission *ad gentes*. We set out toward the others bearing in our body the dying of Jesus.[411] Above all, his love for us, full of mercy and goodness, without judgment…

405. Zeal.
I went with my heart in my hand,
walking,
and blood dripped
on my feet:
It was his blood,
and I stopped
and I gave the news of his love,
of his heart, of his blood.
I don't know if he listened to me,
but I knew that it was true,
it was his heart.

406. Today, June 2, 2006, Vigil of the Feast of Pentecost. With Pope Benedict XVI toward the world. We finished the convivence of the communities *ad*

---
[410] Cf. 1 Cor 15:51.
[411] Cf. 2 Cor 4:10.

gentes. Seven new communities depart with their presbyters to the non-Christians, the unbaptized. We listened to the children of the families and the Lord consoled us: a miracle, families with 10 or 12 or 13 grown children, all in the Church, all disposed to leave everything and to depart with their parents to the unbaptized, in an *implantatio ecclesiae*, showing what a Christian community is, the body of the risen Christ... How can I not give you glory? I can only say to you, my Jesus, "Depart from me, Lord, for I am a sinful man!"[412]

407. In a cave in Moratalla, near Caravaca de la Cruz, August 23, 2006.
Do not abandon me, Lord. Have mercy on me, for I am a sinner.
"Return to me the joy of salvation. Do not thrust me far from your face. Do not take from me your Holy Spirit."[413]

And in this walk,
in this path of troubles,
the soul pressed
and the heart quieted,
the groan of existing...
Oh, who could heal me!
You help me.
Only You remain behind
everything that I am not.

---

[412] Cf. Lk 5:8.
[413] Cf. Ps 51:11-12.

My Lord God,
love of You.
And I, I do what I can.
"Today, convert…!"
Very little is left for me.
"Do not correct me in your anger,
do not punish me in your disdain.
Take pity on me
who have no strength
and my bones are decaying.
My soul is downcast.
And You, Lord, how long?"[414]

408. *Do not withdraw your friendship.*
Oh! How will I be able to live?
If I lack You… Oh, my God!
I am left with almost nothing.
The flour of your love
has been scattered out…
Will I be condemned? Oh!

How is it possible to do the evil that one does not want to do?[415] To love You, Jesus, my love, is the only truth. Awake my soul. Awake! This is the happiest moment of our life: the encounter with You, the *dies natalis*, the day of our death. When will it come? May I not be condemned. Lord, have mercy!

---

[414] Cf. Ps 6:1-3.
[415] Cf. Rom 7:19.

409. I am at the *Domus Galilaeae*. November 24, 2006.
We finished a convivence of the bishops of Asia. From India alone more than 70 came, with a cardinal who surprised everyone with his faith, his discernment and his great simplicity. He does not have the Way and barely knew about it. 18 bishops from the Philippines came as well, along with others from Vietnam, Korea, and one from Japan. In total, 110 bishops. The majority did not know the Way and brought with them a lot of prejudices. The house, the *kerygma*, and, above all, the Holy Land, impressed them. I think that the Lord wants us to help the bishops. He was with us. His Spirit was powerful and wonderful.

410. From the Blessed Charles de Foucauld:
My Father,
I abandon myself to You.
Make of me what you will.
Whatever you make of me,
I give you thanks.
I am disposed to everything,
I will accept anything.
May your will be fulfilled in me,
in all your creatures.
I desire nothing else,
My God.
I place my soul in your hands.
I give it to you, my God,
with all the love in my heart,
because I love You,

> *and the need of this love*
> *is to donate myself,*
> *placing myself in your hands*
> *without reserve,*
> *with infinite trust,*
> *because You are my Father.*
> (Fr. Charles of Jesus)

411. I am in Amsterdam. We begin the mission *ad gentes*. You go before us, we follow You.

412. Today is Holy Saturday, 2007.
     I am spending a day of retreat in a cave in Galilee. It is hot, and, climbing the mountain, I cut my arms on the thorn bushes. Yesterday, I was in Jerusalem, accompanied by Fr. Rino and Carmen. We did the *Via Crucis*. Good Friday on the *Via Dolorosa*.

     > *I am going toward the nothingness of my things,*
     > *I am going amidst the murmur of the waters,*
     > *of the days.*
     > *I go but I remain...*
     > *in the chord of the hours.*
     > *Oh! I am being left with nothing.*
     > *Only your love, which upholds everything,*
     > *Oh! It consoles me.*
     > *And in this being*
     > *and in this staying*
     > *in an existence*
     > *that ends,*
     > *only You,*

> *Jesus Christ,*
> *who care for me,*
> *who love me,*
> *who don't judge me,*
> *who save me.*

413. Lord Jesus, forgive me! My soul almost burns having come close to Hell. Mankind must be saved from Hell, from the horrible Hell. How horrible was what I felt!

414. "Mercy, Lord, mercy. Because of your great goodness, because of your immense compassion,"[416] Lord, help me, help us. Come!

415. *I went with the heart in my hand,*
    walking,
    and drops of blood
    were running over my feet.
    And it was his blood because of that people,
    because of that street,
    because of all mankind,
    because of the women
    and because of me.
    Woe is me
    if I do not announce the Gospel![417]

---

[416] Cf. Ps 51:1.
[417] Cf. 1 Cor 9:16.

416. In a grotto in the mountains of Moratalla, in Murcia, close to Caravaca. In the silence, the wind that blows, a bird that sings and the wind blows through the trees outside. The depths of my being worn out, my sins weigh on me, I have lost self-esteem. I want to love You… I have been alone here for hours. Where are You? My Jesus, come! Have mercy on me, Lord. Help me not to doubt You, your love for me.
Yes! You are so good to me: the Way, the Pope, the *Statutes*, Carmen who corrects me… Oh, holy humility of Christ, who could find you!

417. I am at the Synod of Bishops on the Word of God. The Pope has named me an "auditor." I feel my soul dark and my sins weigh on me. Lord, do not withdraw your grace from me, your friendship. Without You, what shall I do? I ask your forgiveness. Help me!

418. "Without Me, you can do nothing."[418] Without You, I cannot, Lord, have mercy. I must do penance and I have no strength. Without you, everything can crumble. Sustain it! Oh! Who will help me? Woe is me, who suffer your absence! Come! Don't leave me! Where can I go? You alone hold the depths of my being, the deepest part. Grip my soul, O Lord.

---

[418] Cf. Jn 15:5.

419. *In the depths of my being,*
the deepest part,
there where your image is reflected…
You made me like You…
"Man and woman He made them."[419]
And in your reflection
I learn your resemblance,
I learn your will:
your image.
To be in You
and in the immense fire of You
and of your love,
among galaxies,
in an immeasurable universe…
Oh! Have mercy, Lord.

420. We finished the convivence with the bishops of Europe in the *Domus Galilaeae*. Today is April 7, 2008. I am in Rome. And I am a sinner. The Lord was with us. He carried the convivence. Nine cardinals and 170 bishops came. We inaugurated the little monastery. In the center, there is a chapel for the perpetual adoration of the Body of the Lord. I made a sculpture of the Sermon on the Mount as a crown for the chapel. It is made of bronze. The Lord helped me. The Lord is so good to me. He always helps me.

   He and I united for the world, for mankind, for the eternal life gained by Christ for them, for the

---

[419] Gen 1:27.

forgiveness of sins, for his immense compassion. My Lord, Jesus, most beloved Jesus, how can you stand me? I betray you, I am unfaithful, a sinner. You patiently guide me, you care for me, you don't judge me, you love me. And I? Oh, Lord Jesus, have mercy on me, for I am a sinner!

421. June 13, 2008, the Holy Father has definitively approved the *Statute* of the Way. Blessed be the Lord!

422. On January 10, 2009 we will celebrate 40 years of the Way in Rome with the Pope in the Vatican Basilica. On the 9th, the day before, I turn 70. "The Lord is with me like a "powerful warrior."[420] He gives me strength. Live for Him, the rest… What is being, existing, life itself, if not in Him, the true love, love full of eternal light?

423. I am in Sillian, trying to rest. I am 70 years old. It is 2009, July… I write to give You glory. I was at the point of falling, and You did a *surprising miracle* and you saved me and you helped me. Every day is a battle. How I would like to love You. Jesus, my God! Your love and your help surprise me, Lord. May we build the *Domus* in Jerusalem.

424. I am in the mountains of Moratalla, in Murcia, making a day of retreat in a cave. I feel the wind and

---

[420] Cf. Jer 20:11.

my sins weigh on me. Oh! Who will be able to heal me...? Your love pursues me and doesn't leave me for a moment. I must think of You.

I would like to love You. Why do I suffer? My Jesus, to exist in You, to be in You, *one*. This incessant noise, this wind that blows and moans ceaselessly. What will become of me, how will I end up? Help me, Lord! Take pity on me. I take shelter in you; I hold you fast. Lord, have mercy.

425. On the top of this crag, with this incessant wind that surrounds me, gusts that pass like battalions of angels going by. In this loneliness, in this silence resonant with ceaseless moans. In this desire for You, my God! I saw You in the last ones. Oh, holy humility of Christ! And I saw You crucified among the poor. And my life changed. Because your suffering made flesh in the poorest and most miserable of the earth, devours me.

Oh! who can help me?
Give me perfectly Yourself,
send me no more
a messenger
who cannot tell me what I wish..."[421]

Oh! If I could go to the nursing homes and there adore You on my knees in those old people, forgotten and alone, in that orphanage, in the

---

[421] St. John of the Cross, *Spiritual Canticle*.

hospitals, in the prisons full of demons; battered women, abandoned children in the streets, wars full of thousands of sufferings. Hatred, envy, murders, thefts, thefts. Lies, betrayals, incest, adulteries, rapes... Gathered in your flesh, in your body, the sufferings, all caused by evil and sins.

The mystery of You and of your cross is present in the world and calls us to You, to the truth of existence, to crucified love.

426. Oh, holy humility of Christ, who could find you!
I feel my heart is seeking You; it feels attracted to You, in the poor, the poorest, the sick, the elderly, the abandoned children in that orphanage, the crippled, the lame, the old and sick prostitutes, the beggars, the lepers, those who are maltreated in prison, oppressed, abused, raped, those that are dying now, the half-dead soldiers and so many wounded, the last ones, the mentally handicapped, the insane in that asylum... how horrible... the children from those dirty and miserable shacks with still, soulless eyes ... Who stole it from them?

In the suffering of *the innocents* I saw You and was overwhelmed. It was you and things continued regardless. Holy humility of Christ, who could find you! And my life changed, because my heart left to seek you, a deep fire burned in me.

In You life is full, perfect. I need you. My soul thirsts for You.[422] Where are you? Close to the

---

[422] Cf. Ps 42:2.

garbage. Lord Jesus, my God, do not leave me. I am calling You.[423] Dying and finding you more. I'm going, I'm going out to the streets. Wait for me, Lord.

427. Save me, Lord, for I will be lost. I am afraid; the devil prowls around trying to devour me.[424] How will I be able to escape from his trap? You, you will help me.
Have mercy on me! May I love you above all things, Jesus, my God.

428. O Jesus, my love, do not leave me! Do not take your Spirit away from me. Have mercy on me. Help me. If I lack your love, your friendship, your consolation, where shall I go? What will I do?
O my God, have mercy! I would like to fast, and I cannot. I would like to be temperate... Woe is me! I would like to be... It is You who are.[425]
I must accept dying, getting old, without strength, without breath, and without You... Woe is me! Lord, come! My Jesus! Not to doubt ever of your love.

429. 1. Hail Mary, resplendent as the sun.
2. Hail Mary, pillar of fire that shows the way.

---

[423] Cf. Ps 141:1.
[424] Cf. 1 P 5:8.
[425] Cf. Ex 3:14.

3. Hail Mary, hope of the ends of the earth. You are the only uncorrupt dove, the burning bush that is not consumed.

4. Hail Mary, guardian angel of the third millennium. You intercede for the whole human race. Humble and holy Mary, all the beauty of the Spirit is in you: "glory" that in the world makes every creature beautiful.

5. Hail Mary, bulwark of weak souls, phylactery of perfect chastity, most perfumed ark of the Holy Spirit.[426]

To you we pray for all men: give the Church a new ardor for holiness and grace to make a New Evangelization fertile; help the Holy Father and help us all, for we are sinners. AMEN.

430. Little and hidden Mother of Jesus, silent and obedient. You alone have been able to bear the suffering of the innocent in the horror of the death of your Son. Your soul has been pierced by the clanging sword:[427] white-hot flame of the angel of death?

Oh, pierced-through tower,
breeched!
Oh, tower of love,
with your Son you were
annihilated, reduced

---

[426] From a hymn of Roman the Melodist.
[427] Cf. Lk 2:35.

to nothing for me...!

431. *"The genius leaves his trace
like the hare leaves its footprints on the snow.
So...
So the world stops in waiting for
some hare to run across improbable snowfalls."*[428]

432. *I go and things
continue, unmoved.
I go toward You,
toward You, my Lord God.
And contemplating the indifference
in this infinity of still instants...
I would like to penetrate the veil.
I am in this existing.
I am, I exist... I go
toward You.
Why do I suffer?
I feel that existence
thickens and becomes solid.
It is difficult to walk
and toward You I go...*

433. I search over and over in the history of my life. I search for You. You are surprising in me. I was among the poor, I was. And when I see someone suffering, I think, poor thing... and I don't know how to help them. By being close. "I am here,

---

[428] Cf. Eugenio Montale, "The Genius."

courage!" You came to the earth and clothed yourself in humility. Oh, holy humility of Christ, who could find you!

434. *And contemplating the indifference*
and things continue, unmoved.
And You, my Lord God.
Oh! And walking
toward the nothingness of things.
And continuing and continuing to live
Waiting for You.
If I look at myself and enter within myself…
Who am I?
And my life, what a mystery.
I'm going! Here I come,
wait for me, dead ones,
who are in the tombs:
dry bones,
ashes, dust…
Open, oh heavens!

435. "And then he withdrew from them about a stone's throw, knelt down, and prayed: 'Father, if you are willing, take this cup from me; yet, not my will but yours be done.' Then an angel from heaven appeared to him and gave him strength. In his anguish he prayed more earnestly, and his sweat became like great drops of blood falling down on the ground."[429]

---

[429] Lk 22:41-44.

> "And going a little farther, he threw himself on the ground and prayed that, if it were possible, the hour might pass from him. He said, 'Abba, Father, for you all things are possible; remove this cup from me; yet, not what I want, but what you want.'"[430]

436. We have returned from Shanghai. We were in Washington and in Japan.... In Shanghai, in the parish of St. Francis Xavier, we made a great altarpiece in gold with the second coming of Christ and the *Crown of Mysteries*. You helped us. What can I say? We suffered a lot in Japan. It is necessary to love the enemy... who detests us.

> "*Return, dove,*
> *for the wounded deer*
> *appears on the hill!*"[431]
> *The effort of the days, of the years,*
> *of being here when You leave...*

437. Do not withdraw your grace from me, do not take away your Holy Spirit. Have mercy on me, for I am a sinner. Without You... where shall I go? I can do nothing; I die. Woe is me, for You leave me because of my sins! Grant me conversion. Help me, I have no strength! How can I go on?
Zeal is the *essence* of the fire of the Holy Spirit. The essence of God is his love, his burning desire for

---

[430] Mk 14:35-36.
[431] St. John of the Cross, *Spiritual Canticle*.

our salvation. Save us from Hell, from pain and death, from the infinitely dark not-being, from the bottomless, eternal pit... Oh! Who could heal me! Give me of the zeal of your love. Let us go out to the fields, go out the crossroads, to the byways, the cities, and beg men on our knees to accept forgiveness, reconciliation, "In the name of God, we exhort you: reconcile with God," says St. Paul.[432] "For our sake he made him to be sin who knew no sin, so that in him we might become *the righteousness of God*."[433]

Let us not make the blood of God poured out for us be in vain. Oh God, You are my God! Have mercy! You filled my soul with compassion and I shudder when I think of the poor, of the crippled, of the elderly abandoned in nursing homes, prisons, the homeless lying in the streets, the children, so many orphans, alone, the sick... "Blessed are the poor, for the kingdom of heaven is theirs."[434]

It is hot, and more than 100,000 young people await us. The Holy Father is here. How much longer do I have, Lord? Raise us up! Let us go to the world proclaiming your love and salvation. Call many young people. China awaits us. Asia calls us. And, in their slavery, men continue to search among the garbage for a little consolation in life. What a mystery! But You have come. You have already

---

[432] Cf. 2 Cor 5:20.
[433] 2 Cor 5:21.
[434] Cf. Mt 5:3.

arrived. And You come and You come to us. Have mercy on me.

Friday, August 19, 2011.

438. It is hot, so hot... We shall sing. Mary, Mary, Mother of God! We will play, if you help us, a symphony that shows your love and that of your Mother. The suffering of the innocent. The innocent Lamb. Gethsemane. And an angel came to comfort him. He couldn't bear it any longer. Abba, Father![435]

439. Jesus, have mercy. I only know as I am known.[436] Your love in me, what a mystery. The truth, goodness, beauty, love...
Be careful with the workings of your body, lest you find yourself doing what you should not do.
Only in You does my being expand and embrace every creature. Why? Your love consumes me. Divorces, divorces, so many destroyed children... families broken. What can we do? It seems to me that we move too slowly. Islam is expanding... "Zeal for your house consumes me."[437] Have mercy!

440. *And in this being of You and of death,*
and in these endless pains,
in this veil of transparencies,

---

[435] Cf. Lk 22:42-44.
[436] Cf. 1 Cor 13:12.
[437] Cf. Ps 69:9; Jn 2:17.

> *full of weakness... I say to myself:*
> *Woe is me!*
> *Who will heal me?*
> *Do not leave me.*
> *In this sea of your absence,*
> *in this walking toward death*
> *in this aging*
> *and in this deep being*
> *in the constant memory of your love...*
> *that love that marked my life*
> *forever...*
> *I constantly cry out: Where are You?*

441. I already see the city in the distance, although I still have hills to climb. Oh! Let me draw a breath... The thought is constantly with me: if you take away your grace, if you withdraw your friendship, your love, and your presence... Oh! How can I go on? "Do not correct me in your anger, do not chastise me. Look at me, for I lack strength. My bones are all broken. My soul is downcast. And You, Lord, how much longer?" says the Psalm.[438]

    Oh, what pain! Old age, sickness, and death. Oh, what pain! Loneliness, so many people in nursing homes, retirement homes, hospitals... Alone, moored to existence, in a wheelchair. And life escapes us... quietly, and to live is to die.

    "You made yourself like me, Jesus, my God, so that I would not be afraid to encounter you; your face

---

[438] Cf. Ps 6:1-3.

like mine, so that I could love You.[439] And, made man, You humbled yourself through obedience[440] to life, to the sin of men who envied You and hated You; they did not want you: "Away with him! Away with him! Crucify him!"[441]

Oh, what pain!
Resurrexit!
Resurrexit!

Come to me, Lord Jesus, resurrected from pain, from death and from sin.

442. From the depths of my being, the deepest part, I cry: Where are you? If you take away your friendship, your grace, your presence… what will I do? Where will I go? What is life without You? And walking toward death… But, no! You are present. You always helped me. My whole history is redolent with your love and your presence. I will pour out my history so that people will see You, my God. Holy, holy, holy, God Sabaoth! If I lack you, Lord, where can I go? Come, my God! Come. Help me!

443. Lord Jesus, if You are lacking, what will I do? If You withdraw from me, how will I be able to survive, how will I go on? I lack strength.

---

[439] Cf. *Ode of Solomon*, VII.
[440] Cf. Phil 2:8.
[441] Jn 19:15.

And in this walking
with almost no strength,
on this path
of pains…
You, my Lord God,
do not leave me.
Come, for I die without You!
Only You and your love.
I have nothing left.
Help me!
Hold me tight, tight.
Embrace me, love me.
Lord, come!

444. Lord! In this walking among pains, in this being of You, between my I and myself, my being moves and my existence walks… What is happening to me? My life is an instant that passes… Oh, what pain, do not leave me! No, do not withdraw from me. Do not take away from me the feeling of You. My life is You, and to die is to be with You: a great gain and better by far.[442]

Why do *I exist in the love for the others*? And those who are alone, what horror.

You are in the suffering of the innocent, in so many victims, because You are the love for everyone, for the poor, for us. My Jesus and my Lord, come, do not delay, help me!

---

[442] Cf. Phil 1:23.

And in what happened yesterday, first, and in this slow slipping and sliding toward death, the constant thought of You and of your absence... Oh, who will heal me! And in this walking amid troubles, toward You, toward you I go, Lord, my God.

445. Feeling and feeling You, my God. And in the distance, that Beast who moves in the abyss and wants to get out to consume us.[443] Oh, if You were not! Oh, what pain! But, no, You are, and You love us. What a great mystery is the love that You have for us. Yes, crucified, Lamb without blemish, sweet and silent, brought to the slaughter and there slit and killed... And they are killing You, and You are saving us. From evil, taken on in your flesh, you take out the supreme good.

446. December 29, 2011.
I am in Jerusalem. Yesterday, December 28, 2011, on the Feast of the Holy Innocents, we had a concert in Jerusalem, the symphony, with the Jews. At the beginning, there was a lot of tension, especially when I said that it would be a "symphonic-catechetical" celebration. The presiding rabbi was fantastic. It was as though he was conscious that the "Messiah" was nearing. At the end, a Jewish woman who is a Holocaust scholar and was deeply moved told me that rivers of blood

---

[443] Cf. Rev. 11:7.

from the Nazi concentration camps had converged for the meeting that night in Jerusalem.

447. Today, January 6, 2012.
I get up and I say, "My soul is thirsting for You."[444] Oh! Who could save me? Come, Lord Jesus! How can I go on? Grant me, Lord, contrition, compunction, the remembrance of You with tears, knowledge of myself, of my faults, of my sins, of how I am. Make me aware of death, of my own death, give me humility, help me to be temperate, give me love for You and for mankind, give me, Lord, tenderness of heart, your tenderness, that You have for those who suffer, for the poor. Oh, holy humility of Christ, who could find you! Divine tenderness, love in the heart. Why am I moved by man?

448. "They are not grieved over the ruin of Joseph,"[445] said the Rabbi in Jerusalem. In the music, he felt our compassion and was surprised. Is it the Messiah who is approaching them in us, those whom God loves so much? "Despised, rejected by all men..."[446] It is always the "Servant" in them, the Messiah who fills the world. The same sap moves us, in the one olive tree.[447]
And in this event and in this being of You and of things, I go, I walk slowly toward You. Toward

---

[444] Ps 63:1.
[445] Cf. Am 6:6.
[446] Is 53:3.
[447] Cf. Rom 11:17.

death? Yes, toward You. You in the depths of my being. I am, yes, I feel myself, I am in You and I live and... how much longer do I have? I feel my soul recollected in your now, You who give me life. And life is a relationship, it is a dialogue with You. If I lose you, I die.

Art is a relationship of love, each thing sings the beauty of that which is alongside it,[448] as if saying, "Live, courage, for I will help you." Love is a relationship; art is a relationship. Life is a relationship with time, with things, with others, who look at us and who are present. It is a relationship with God, with the deepest part of you... with your history.

And contemplating indifference. And things continue unmoved. And I am embraced by time, carried... toward death. If I could pass through the darkness and find myself with You. Yes, cloud and darkness surround You.[449] Lord, Jesus, dear brother, my Lord and my God, have mercy on me!

449. I've turned 73, and the Pope has approved the celebrations that mark the steps of Christian Initiation in the Way, celebrations that are in the *Catechetical Directory of the Neocatechumenal Way*. How good you are, Lord! I do not understand. You have allowed me to compose a symphony to the Blessed Virgin Mary about the suffering of the innocent.

---

[448] Cf. Sir 42:25.
[449] Cf. Ps 97:2.

We performed it in Jerusalem for the Jews. So many miracles! It was a symphonic-catechetical celebration in which the Word and the music are listened to, and they pray. Miracles and conversions.

450. We are going to India, and Carmen is not well. Help her and heal her! Help me to love you, Lord!

451. I don't know if I should publish these pages. "Never stop doing good for fear of vanity; that comes from the devil." Yes, it's true, I am afraid of vanity, the attacks, that they will say I'm trying to play the saint, when the truth is that… Am I vain? Do good, nothing else matters.

452. May 1, 2012.
By that dark path,
by the hidden path,
by the disguised ladder,
in that sorrow
that pains my heart…
Oh, what anguish, what pain!
Those bed-ridden old people,
who looked and looked at me
moving their eyes…
Oh, compassion, compassion
that comes close and wounds me!
Oh, holy humility of Christ!
Take pity on me,
for I am a sinner.
And in this walking and walking

toward death,
Gather me into Yourself,
do not leave me…

453. We made a trip through America holding concerts. The first in the Boston Symphony Hall. It was fantastic. The symphonic-catechetical celebration was presided by Cardinal O'Malley.

    Afterward, we went to New York, where we held the concert in Avery Fisher Hall at the Lincoln Center, which is one of the most prestigious concert halls in the world. About 30 Rabbis and more than 2,500 Jews attended, as we wanted to perform the symphony for the Jews of New York. The reception was fantastic. We all sang, standing, and many crying, "Shema, Israel." Numerous rabbis told us that it was the first time that the Catholic Church paid homage to the Holocaust. They invited us to play the symphony in an orthodox synagogue. It was wonderful.

    Next, we had a meeting in Chicago with more than 10,000 brothers and sisters. We called for vocations for Asia and everything was wonderful. 300 boys, more than 200 girls and some 500 families stood up for the mission. Afterward, thousands of young people offered themselves to pray the rosary every day before the Blessed Sacrament for the mission *ad gentes*. We held the concert in the Symphony Center of Chicago. It was full, packed. There was an amazing attention and enthusiasm there.

This trip bringing the music of the suffering of the innocents is Jesus in the Garden of Olives, sustained and helped by an angel, and the Blessed Virgin at the foot of the cross, placed before the scandal of the suffering of the Innocent One, punished, without fault, deformed by the blows of those who hate him... and his poor Mother there, while a sword pierces her heart.[450]

You have placed in our hearts a great love for your people, Israel. I don't know what you want from us. Oh, if You lifted the veil...! Help me to be humble, so that they may see You in me and come near...

454. Do not desire that life be like you think It should be... Let everything be as God wills... After your Baptism, you are no longer god. God is He, who leads your history and guides you to heaven. You no longer live in yourself? Then you are Christian.

455. *I go toward the nothingness of my things,*
I go amidst the babbling of the waters,
of the days,
I go and I stay
In the chords of the hours.
Oh! With nothing I remain.
Only your love, which upholds everything,
consoles me.

---

[450] Cf. Jn 19:25, Lk 2:35.

456. Today, August 14, 2012.
I am in the cave of Moratalla. I would like to remain some hours with You, Lord Jesus, in silence and with the howling wind, which comes and goes, and I tremble as I think of You, of your love, of your election, of the many things we have done together...

Who am I? Everything that You did with me. My living was You, Lord. It is so surprising... I don't know if it was me. In Africa, in that whorehouse wanting to rescue a minor. In Berta's house. After that, in the shantytown... the fear of death, Mariano, drunk so many nights, Joaquin and Antonia, Jose Agudo and Rosario, Santiago, Felipe, Basilio, and many, many more, Julianita, Sir Juan, who slept in the garbage, Carmen "number two," Mariano's wife, Manolo, Flor, who stayed with Carmen in her shack, and Domingo, and *Chulo Maletas,* "the Cool One on crutches" who begged for alms in the Metro... afterward came el Niño, Tito, Antonio, Enrique the gypsy... and your constant presence.

457. It was, perhaps, mid-November when I approached the shantytown of Palomeras.
Sleeping like a puppy lying under a cart. Sleeping and waking at dawn, close to the path, beside my shack. He was a tinker: blonde, young, recently married... I was so close to the earth that I was almost inside it, and it felt good to be there.

The dogs that kept me warm, the tinkers, Joaquin, Antonia, Sir Juan... My shack made of boards full of holes was on the side of the path that rose toward the fountain, which was 500 meters further up, among the lower houses of Palomeras Altas. The gypsies and tinkers, who lived in the caves that were below, 200 meters from our shacks, had to pass in front of my shack every day going for water. Soon, everyone knew me: the guitar, the cross on the wall, the Bible, my bearded face...

I don't know how to write this story. It seems to diminish it, make it smaller. The Lord led me, and He lived through me events that are unspeakable, of joy, of the love of God, of fear, of anguish... of the presence of the Lord Jesus. Christ was present there. Everything spoke of Him. I and He one, perfectly one.

The dogs, so many dogs always accompanied me. I looked like a shepherd with his sheep, but, no, they were dogs. I crossed *Colonia Sandi* every morning at eight to take the bus; everyone stared at me, seeing me with so many dogs, and I didn't know what to do.

One time, the Lord used the dogs so that I would learn to humble myself. I taught classes in the morning at a school that was very far away. I always had to take three modes of transportation: the bus in *Colonia Sandi*, which took me to the Metro, in Vallecas; the Metro to Atocha; and in Atocha Plaza a trolley that took me to the school. I almost always arrived late, so the principal of the school had to substitute for me in class until I arrived. The last time I arrived late, about 20 minutes behind schedule, because of the bus or something I can't remember, the principal was so angry that he yelled at me in front of all my students. I promised him it wouldn't happen again and asked his forgiveness in front of the kids. I taught drawing classes. The kids were 11 or 12 years old, children of low-class people; they loved me a lot. I always spoke to them of God and the Bible.

Though in the shantytown everything was very chaotic, with Mariano who almost always arrived drunk and I had to listen to him, etc., after that violent tongue-lashing, the next day I got up half an hour early: I absolutely had to arrive on time.

I washed quickly and set off running through the field toward *Colonia Sandi* to catch the bus, when I noticed the dogs were running with me. There were about 15 of them. One of the dogs must have been in heat; the other dogs were trying to get close to her. When I arrived at the bus stop, the people complained. "So many dogs!" they said, "But where do they come from?" I pretended I had no idea, hoping the bus would arrive. Finally, it arrived. I got on quickly and sat in the back. I sighed with relief, thinking I would arrive on time, when I looked out the back window and saw the 15 dogs running behind the bus. My God! I was done for! I pushed my way to the front of the bus – which, as always, was full of laborers going to work – to be the first one off so the dogs wouldn't see me and enter the Metro.

The bus arrived at the Metro station. I joined the crush of people without looking behind me. I got my ticket and leaped down the endless stairs three at a time. As I reached the platform, I was quite nervous, hoping the train would arrive soon. I glanced out of the corner of my eye at the large staircase leading to the platform and watched in horror as the 15 dogs came running down it. As soon as they saw me, they raced to greet me, jumping for joy.

The station boss blew his whistle. The police came; they detained me and made me leave the Metro station with all the dogs, accompanied by the police. It was absolutely forbidden to bring animals there. The dogs happily joined me climbing the stairs. It was useless to insist they weren't mine…

And so, I was late again. I arrived at the school so humiliated that when the principal saw me, he didn't say a word. What a face I must have had! I offered it to the Lord because I thought He must have used the dogs to teach me to humble myself.

When I think about the dogs, I get emotional: they were so good to me. They had never followed the bus. But that time they did. What a mystery…

On the subject of humiliation, another surprising event happened to me another time. We were in the shantytown. Carmen had spoken to me about a professor of liturgy who explained the Council's renewal, and said I should hear him. She attended his classes at the Pastoral Institute Leo XIII, which was on the outskirts of Madrid in *Ciudad Universitaria.*

Living in the shacks, I always dressed the same: in black, with a parka and black corduroy pants, with a beard, etc. When I arrived at the Pastoral Institute after a very long trip, because my shack was on the other end of the city, thinking I was arriving late, I went running in and crossed the entrance hall. There was a large staircase and a uniformed porter sitting behind a table to the right of the staircase.

I passed in front of the porter and climbed the stairs three at a time. Suddenly, I heard the porter shout behind me, "Hey! Hey! You!... Thief! Thief!" The end of the staircase turned and led to a vestibule. The exact moment I arrived, the bell rang signaling the end of class, and a bunch of priests and nuns exited the rooms, while behind me, the porter climbed the stairs with great effort, shouting, "Thief! Thief!" I stopped and said, "Are you talking to me?" "Yes, you!" Meanwhile, priests and nuns were bumping into me all around. The porter continued to shout, "Who are you? How did you get in here? Call the police! Call the dean!" Everything was chaos, and a murmur was heard, "What is going on?" "They caught a thief!"

During all this, the dean of the Institute arrived, all in a hurry. It was Monsignor Guix, who was later named Auxiliary Bishop of Barcelona, and then Bishop of Vic, in Catalonia. I knew him: after they had awarded me the Extraordinary National Prize in painting, I was once invited to form part of the jury for an oil painting exposition-contest in a Catholic college, and there we met because he was also part of the jury. Because of this, when I saw him, I breathed a sigh of relief, thinking he would remember me. I didn't realize how different I looked from then: now I had a beard, was unkempt, dressed all in black, fairly dirty..., etc.

When the porter came and gave his explanation, they let me speak, while all around I could hear the whispering of the priests and nuns who were jostling me, and I said nervously to the director, "Don't you remember me? We met each other in a "trial"! Instead of saying, "jury of art [*jurado*]," I said, "trial [*juicio*]." And he said, "I don't know you! I've never been on trial with you! Throw him out of here!"

I said that I had been invited by Carmen Hernandez, that she wanted... It was useless. The porter and the others grabbed me and threw me out. As soon as they closed the main door behind me, I saw Carmen arriving happily, shouting from afar, "Kiko, let's go in quickly because the class is going to start!" I told her that I wasn't going in there again. Before I could say anything else, she grabbed me by the arm and pushed me up the entrance stairway again.

I was telling her, "They just mistook me for a thief and kicked me out!" She wouldn't listen.

"Come on, come on!" she shouted at me.

In the end, I thought, "Lord, what do you want from me? To go in again? May everything be for love of You." And like a lamb brought to the slaughter, I again climbed the entrance stairs behind Carmen. When the porter saw me, he understood that he had made a mistake and said nothing more. Later, I found out that the day before, the institute had been robbed and they had scolded the porter thoroughly.

I listened to Msgr. Farnés' liturgy class, and I liked it.

458. I had to start working as a construction worker building roads. My shack was full of young men released from prison, coming from drugs. Impressed by me, they wanted to live with me and no longer stole. I thought: if I begin to work, they will come with me. And so it was.

I met Jorge in the time of the Cursillos and knew he had a company that laid and repaired highways, and that they were currently working in the neighborhood of Aluche. He hired me and nine of the young men, as well as Jose Agudo. The foreman put me and another guy on the concrete mixer. The carts came for us to fill. It was my job to shovel in sand. The other guy who was with me shoveled in gravel and cement.

After three hours with the shovel, my hands were cut and began to bleed. When the other guy saw it, he told me, "Don't worry. I'll do your job." And so he did. We became friends. He was an ex-soldier. I spoke to him of Christ, and he was very impressed.

He wanted to come with me to the shantytown. And I couldn't say no to him.

While we were talking in my shack, I began to think about Mariano, who came every night high on drugs and liquor, and who, before leaving for his own hut, near mine, came in and I would have to listen to him. He talked and talked, and I couldn't move or show annoyance because he would become furious. He was extremely violent.

And indeed, he arrived half drunk, as always, and I introduced the others, and he began to talk and talk. After an hour, the ex-soldier told him, "Ok enough, tomorrow at six, we have to get up to go to work." Mariano, as if he hadn't heard, continued to talk. At that point, the ex-soldier stood up and yelled, "I said enough! Now, go!" Mariano didn't say a word, got up and left for his hut.

I followed him. I knew he was going to look for his knife. He came out of his shack in a fury and told me, "Out of the way, I'm going to rip that guy right now!" I tried to move closer, and he took a swipe at me with a very large knife. I dodged it, and it whooshed past me very close. Then I held him and managed to take away the knife. He took off running. I went toward my shack. The ex-soldier was behind the door with an iron bar, and he said to me, "If that guy comes in, I'll kill him. I know his type. I was in the Seventh Ward of the prison. Did you see how he was rubbing his hands?"

I told the ex-soldier, "And now what do we do? Because I think that this isn't over. He went to look for a gas can. Since this hut is against the hillside, he can sprinkle it and light us on fire from above. Wait here. I'm going to see if I can find him." Finally, I found him, and he cried and cried.

All ended well, but the Lord, with this fact, allowed me to experience the fear of death. Every night as I approached my hut, my legs trembled. While Mariano talked and talked, I held my knees so that he wouldn't see my terror. The devil made me think that Mariano would kill me and then commit suicide, that was what he wanted because he said that I was what he most loved in the world. But the Lord helped me. What fear I experienced…!

459. *I would like to be, and to be in You*
dawn of certainty,
of light of incorruptible life,
of eternal life.
With the mind certain
and the soul pressed,
in a you that is closed
more and more in You,
My Jesus…
Love, your love for me,
total, absolute, infinite,
full of tenderness and compassion.
You are certain, Lord.
I would like to be, and to be in You
dawn of love,
of eternal life.

460. I would like to be, crying, that poet who sings and sings your infinite compassion, your tenderness, your pain, for mankind. You have wounded my heart, which feels the suffering of so many poor people in your infinite compassion... Jailer, jailer closing the bars, once again you are closing the hard iron bars of the prisons... where outcasts drag themselves through a life marked by the evil of others... What a mystery evil is! Why? Men rob, they lie, they commit adultery, they kill, they commit suicide... with their reason gone mad and their souls downcast.

461. *By the hidden path,*
in that dark jungle,
by the secret disguised ladder
of a thousand sighs of love,
with a wounded soul...
Oh, Jesus, take pity on me!
If You leave me and You go
What will become of me?
Either You or Hell.
Forgive me,
for I am very weak,
for I am a sinner...
Let us tighten the bonds of mutual love,
let us embrace each other in the Spirit.
Make me one,
perfectly one, in You.
And in this walking and walking,

> *among weaknesses and betrayals,*
> *with an abyss on my right*
> *and a precipice on my left,*
> *I go.*
> *Help me, for I can do no more*
> *than live groaning!*

462. November 17, 2012

    I am in a small grotto near Tabgha, facing the Sea of Galilee. They say it's one of the possible sites where the Lord climbed the mountain to pray all night.[451] There is a stone with an inscription memorializing this.

    I am trying to pray and to speak with You. What a great mystery life is. You gave me a sensitive heart that feels your infinite compassion for those who suffer, the poor, the imprisoned, the sick, the abandoned children in orphanages, the oppressed... The mystery of human suffering, the suffering of the innocents... Oh, how I would like to kneel and to console, heal, tell them how much You love them. You made yourself like them. You tore the evil out of suffering, which is sin.[452] You took the power over death from the devil. You saved us from "not being" and from nothingness, from Hell, which is where You are not. How I would like to love You! My Jesus, come, help me!

---

[451] Cf. Lk 6:12.
[452] Cf. 1 Cor 15:56.

463.   July 17, 2013.
Only a word to give thanks to God for the symphony we performed in Auschwitz. It was wonderful. Before the Gate of Death, about 70 rabbis from all over the world, 6 cardinals, some 80 bishops and more than 13,000 brothers and sisters. All together sang the *"Shema."* It was wonderful. Also hearing the *"Resurrexit"* there, in that place of death and horror, of disdain for God and man...

After, we went to Lublin, where the University granted me a doctorate *honoris causa* in theology. I do not wish for flattery and honors, but rather, disdain and persecution. I accepted it because I think that, behind it, they wanted to recognize the good that the Way is doing in Poland, where there are more than 1,400 communities.

We also held the concert in Lublin Square, in front of the castle where so many Poles and Jews were tortured and died. There something surprising happened. It occurred to me that morning, before the concert, as in many other places, to do an exorcism in that same square in front of the castle, cursing the devil to leave the city... I think that the devil became angry, because during the catechetical symphony a torrential rain was unleashed. The whole square was full of people, even the green areas, which made a kind of basin. No one moved, with so many umbrellas. But suddenly the person responsible for the sound and lights said that everything had to be turned off, the lights, etc. They turned off our microphones. There was danger of a huge short-circuit, and that a fire would start, etc. We all waited for the rain to stop, but no, it went on an on. We started to sing songs of the Way without microphones. The lead technician was very impressed that so many bishops and rabbis and so many people, completely soaked, did not move. Everyone stayed in his place. In the end, the technician responsible turned on the lights and sound and we were able to begin again, in the rain. The devil did not succeed in cancelling the symphonic-catechetical celebration; on the contrary, it was marvelous. Everyone standing and singing "*Shema-Israel.*" A moment of true brotherhood between Catholics and Jews, a moving moment for so many Poles who in the last war were despised. God made himself present. I will never forget it.

Afterward, we went to Budapest, to play the symphony in the Opera House, full of Hungarians and Jews. Everything went very well.

When we sang the "*Shema,*" the Jews, who were half the audience, put on their *kippahs.*

Lord, what do you want of us?

464. The glory of man is nothing. Nothing has value without humility.

465. I am in Sillian (Austria), July 22, 2013.
I have to leave for Brazil, Rio de Janeiro, for World Youth Day with the new Pope, Francis. I am approaching the veil. I already feel what is behind

it. And the evil that filters through startles me. Is it the apostasy? Is it the antichrist? And the tremendous mystery surprises me… that God accepted to be removed from the world and be taken out of the city, like trash is taken out… and they killed him. Each person can remove God from their life, can kick him out, what a mystery…

They expel us from the world, and the Jews as well. They kicked them out of the cities and brought them to die, what a mystery… evil in the world. I live submerged in these mixed thoughts, and who am I? How can I judge? I am a sinner. What a mystery… sin, doing the evil that, deep down, one does not want to do.[453] Man, is he poor? Weak? Small? He is big enough to kick God out of his home, to tell God, "I don't need you. Out!"

466. Oh, holy humility of Christ, who could find you! O holy humility of the heart of Christ, sweet love, gentle rest that doesn't resist evil. You are the luminous garment of the true Christian. You are the eternal sweetness of the crucified Lord. Oh, holy humility of Christ, who could find you!

467. The quality of a Christian is seen and recognized in temptations. Yes, I go from one to the next, I leave one and expect the next. "Oh, if you only knew the gift of God and who it is that says to you, 'Give me

---

[453] Cf. Rom 7:19.

to drink'!"⁴⁵⁴ Oh, the living water of your love! What a mystery that Christ is God. Crucified in Him, God himself reveals his humility, goodness. Without bitterness, he shouts, "Forgive them!"⁴⁵⁵ Oh, what a mystery that man could kill God, within himself, that he could expel him and commit adultery, rob, lie, and kill!

468. I am again in the cave of Moratalla. Today is August 24, 2013.
I have been reading the Letter to the Colossians. How great St. Paul is, what great inspiration, what love for Christ, what a great gift to the Church. And I… how can I not bless you and give you thanks for your infinite compassion? Why do I live in a groan? My living is groaning. I awake and shout, "Come, help me!"

469. *Groaning and groaning as I live*
and You have squeezed my heart,
You tighten it and press it
and you make me groan and groan…
What a mystery it is to be,
to exist, to live.
The days are already dwindling,
the silent nights are already passing,
and they slip out under the door.
And time before me, unmoved.

---

⁴⁵⁴ Cf. Jn 4:10.
⁴⁵⁵ Cf. Lk 23:34.

And in this resounding loneliness I exist,
I exist with You.
Yes, with You to exist, to be,
and to die with You.

470. May zeal for your love invade my heart so that I may set out. Convivences, announcement of the kerygma, 20,000 priests for China. India, Laos, Cambodia, Vietnam... Indonesia, Borneo, millions and millions of people who do not know You. Marx, Engels and Lenin are apostles of the antichrist; they have immersed humanity in an anthropology that is a lie. What a horror are communism and its consequences: atheism, corruption, worship of money, prostitution, deceit...

Jesus, my Lord God, let us go out to the world and to mankind, we will bring them your love, your death and sacrifice, your victory, your light and your glory shining with joy and happiness without end.

The Dragon, the Beast and the false prophet retreat.[456] They are the antichrist of our age... Jesus, lamb without blemish, slaughtered and conqueror upon the heights of our history, with no determinism, in the total freedom you gave to each person. Although today they are slaves, You free them. Blessed be your name!

---

[456] Cf. Rev. 16:13.

La vía del tren, Castilla y una reunión de gít- a 30 metros de la chabola, conmigo y los perros.

471. *And "Upon a dark night*
ablaze with love, with urgent longings,
O happy chance,
I left without being noticed,
My house at last completely quiet."[457]
And in an endless flow of disappointments and groans,
my reason and my soul hidden,
I learned of You.
Oh, what pain to be there,
when a sword
pierces your heart!
I would like to tell You that I love You...
and I go toward the nothingness of my things...
The leaves fall
and I am growing old...
toward You, my Lord God.

472. *Lord, blessed be your name,*
praised through the ages,
blessed forever,
for your great goodness
for your infinite mercy.
In You I was, and in You I am, and in You I shall be.
Because that is your glory:
caring for me, loving me,
who am nothing.
I only exist in You,
in your essence, in your glory.
Lord, my God,

---

[457] St. John of the Cross, *The Dark Night*.

*your love sustains the universe
And all it contains.
We desire love.
"Love one another as I have loved you."*[458]

473. Why is beauty humble? What a mystery! Why is humility so beautiful? I have seen You, Lord. Yes, there You were, in that woman abandoned in the hospital hallway. I saw you lying in the street among cardboard boxes and trash. Oh, holy humility of Christ, who could find you! I found You, and you touched my heart, and I was no longer the same. I wanted to follow You, to find you in prison, to go down to the social hells, among the poor. Where are you? Oh, holy humility of Christ! Let me seek you. Do not leave. Oh, what pain! Come, Lord Jesus! Come!

How is it possible that God has made himself sin…?[459] Total humility. "Awake, Deborah!"[460]

474. Once more I awake to another day of life. One more day toward death. Time is carrying me, impassively… I cannot resist. It surrounds me with its silence, and it is there, inflexible. There is time that leads us toward death. It is silent and empty. It is firm. It is inexorable. It makes us age. How can I redeem time? How can I make its company

---

[458] Cf. Jn 13:34.
[459] Cf. 2 Cor 5:21.
[460] Judg 5:12.

comfort me? Friendly time. You have hidden secretly the meaning of being, of existing, of going toward death.

There is a key that opens you and transforms you and makes you a friend and companion… and that key is You, Lord, my God. You took me out of death and held me tight, clutched me yourself, in your love. I live forever in You. Time means to come closer to You; it is the desire for You, Lord Jesus, my God.

Your will and time… The hell of not knowing. And things continue impassively. And we are going toward nothingness… And You, do not leave me. Have mercy, help me! "If this cup cannot pass without me drinking it, Your will be done, Father… Then an angel from heaven appeared to him, giving him strength."[461]

475. *To live is to groan and groan.*
And to be in You, a shout.
How will I go on?
You have squeezed my soul
With your hands
and I am held tight by You.
Your infinite compassion
for mankind
touched my soul
and is submerged
in a groan of pains.

---

[461] Cf. Mt. 26:42; Lk 22:43.

> *My body, full of pain, contemplates*
> *my groans.*
> *My spirit is frightened,*
> *and silent,*
> *while my soul,*
> *united to You, my Lord God,*
> *deliberates on a mystery*
> *of love for mankind*
> *Courage!*
> *Let us continue, even if we must crawl.*

476. July 2014.

    I have been told to "eat the frog." What a mystery. It's very graphic… And here I am, with no strength, thinking I might die. I don't know how to go on. I must eat the frog. Yes, do not resist evil. Eat the frog. Offer the other cheek, and, even worse, do good to those who hate you. Love the enemy…[462] "Eat the frog." Oh! What pain, and going on toward death with no strength. Lord, help me!

477. Groaning and groaning and shouting like a crazy person. Oh, don't leave me. Oh, for I cannot take it anymore. Oh! In this whimper between painful sighs I go toward the nothingness of my things. And I was left with nothing. What a mystery life is in this existence, to be conscious of the not-being that is death… I only exist in the love for others, for those who suffer, for those who need me.

---

[462] Cf. Mt 5:39,44; Lk 6:27.

478. And in this endlessness of repressed pain, in this being carried by the waters of the days... Who am I? I am a being shaken by life. Am I being dragged by the slow, inexorable current that is carrying me? And faith? Where is my faith in You, my Lord God? Overwhelmed by your longings, you brought me toward the others, you filled my heart with your compassion and I left everything.
And there, among the poor, You lived for me.

479. *And in this being of You and of things,*
I go, abandoned to the time
that carries me slowly
without making itself felt,
while life is becoming
a fatigue that increases
as I pant from the effort.
How will I survive old age,
which inexorably nears?
I am immersed in a temptation
of loneliness and of abandonment of God...

480. *And in this being of You and of things,*
I think you have taken my life
and carried it toward the others.
Why did you pick me?
Who am I?
What a mystery is living and being,
instant after instant, in You,
and in this life without breath,
in the constant memory of You.

> *It is the incommensurable mystery*
> *of You and of your presence.*
> *You emptied me of myself and of your presence,*
> *and without strength I go.*
> *It is You, and things continue impassively.*

481. *On the hidden path,*
in that dark forest,
on the secret ladder of the mighty way
I found you,
disguised by a thousand sighs of love,
the soul wounded.
Nature and time pressed upon me.
And in this grip,
in this combat that age attempts,
silent death…
In the gentle and calm darkness,
it awaits me.
But You, Lord, are near.
You sustain me in the toil of walking.
By the hidden path of the dark forest,
on the disguised ladder I went,
and in the powerful way I found you,
lying in the street, dying of cold.

482. August 15, 2014.
Oh, Jesus, help me, have mercy, I am poor, I am a sinner! How can I go on? My soul is experiencing Your silence. My heart is silent and in pain… and I think, "have You abandoned me?" You hide your face from me and I groan. Groaning and groaning,

living in the constant remembrance of You and of your absence. Who am I? Oh, Jesus, help me to love You. I am in the hell of your absence, tired, having fainted so many times, without the strength to continue… And what will become of me and of the whole Way? You have done so many miracles with us. Lately, the devil is battering us ceaselessly: one suffering after another. And "what can I do if I hope fails me? Offer your cheek to the one who strikes you. Humble yourself, for the Lord is merciful.[463] And with You, walking. Yes, with You.

483. *"The Messiah,*
a lion to conquer,
made himself a lamb to suffer."[464]
And he climbed upon the wood
to be a bridegroom,
to die,
and left his blood,
as a dowry, for his virgin bride.
And he descended into Hell
looking for the lost sheep,
to take Adam from among the dead,
and he rose to heaven,
and at his side seated
the forgiven adulteress,
the cleansed prostitute,
the Church,
bride, virgin, and mother.

---

[463] Cf. Lam 3:18, 30-31.
[464] Cf. Victorinus Petavionensis, *Scholia in Apocalypsin Beati Ioannis*, V.

484. I am in the cave of the mountains of Moratalla, near Caravaca de la Cruz, in Murcia, Spain. Today, August 20, 2014.

I would like to speak with You.
I would like to tell you that I love You.
I would like to be able to pray...
Gusts and gusts of wind.
And You, silent.
In this resounding loneliness,
in the silence of You,
in Your quiet absence,
in the soul's quiet absence.
What do you want of me?
How can I go on?
Come, Lord, come!
Help me.
You are here, and I do not feel You...

485. Woe is me! Lord, take pity on me. Help me!

486. *The painful sighs, certain,*
in an endlessness
of hidden and bewildering
sufferings, the pain
is unspeakable...
But You, Lord, my God...
Being in You,
the fullness of my being,
the deepest part.
Oh! How I would like to love You!

487. *Oh! Who could in You*
be transcendent in love,
be in You, complete One,
the Absolute of being.
To exist dying?
And You, Lord, my God,
do not leave me.
Come! Have mercy.

488. *Forgive me,*
for I can do no more
than groan and groan…
Have mercy, and do not leave me,
do not abandon me
for I will die.
What suffering!
And in this event,
in this being of You and of things,
in this every day, dying.
Help me! Come!
Oh! In this martyrdom
in which You have immersed my soul.
It is hard for me to go on.

489. *How I would like to tell You*
that I love You.
How I would like that…
And in this walking
amid pains…
Oh! How difficult it is for me to live.
Do not go away from me.

Where are You
for I do not feel You?
Why did You go
and leave me alone?
How I would like to tell You
that I love You.

490. *Lord, Jesus, my God,*
do not leave me, for I will be lost.
Look at me, discouraged, with no strength,
descending into the abyss...
Have mercy!
You, always fantastic.
And I? Lost.
Do not leave me!
I shout to You, Lord...
Come to my aid!

491. *And in this living in an endlessness*
of impassive moments,
in crazy coincidence
of dead news,
of sighs and moans,
in a wounded heart...
I think of You, Lord,
and I beg You:
Do not withdraw your love from me,
do not take away your Holy Spirit.[465]

---

[465] Cf. Ps 51:11.

492. *And in this being of You*
and of things,
in this walking
in an immeasurable
weariness,
I don't know, Lord,
if I can go on.
Do not allow my soul
to slip…
And I go
toward the nothingness of things.
And I go
and I am left with nothing.
And when appears before me
the abyss of Hell
that awaits me…
Only You,
in your infinite mercy,
can help me…

493. *Frail, I go,*
my heart dislodged,
my hope consumed,
in this walking
amidst anguish and groans…
You, my God,
do not withdraw from me,
do not leave me.
Come! Help me!
For I can do no more than cry
and tell You that I love You.

494. *Oh! Who could heal me?*
How is it, Lord, that You went away
and left me dying in this living?
If You do not love me
what can I do?
If You do not help me...
I go toward the nothingness of my things
among the murmuring of the waters,
of the days.
I go and I stay
in the chord of the hours
Oh! With nothing.
And when I stand
before You,
Hell, is it waiting for me?
No! You love me,
You help me,
You save me.

495. *And in that endlessness of impassive spaces,*
in that being of those quiet things,
in that existing with the soul immersed,
in a deaf, terrible suffering...
I die. What is happening to me?
Have mercy on me, Lord.
Is it my sins?
Am I left with nothing?
And contemplating indifference
and feeling that I am slipping,
sinking,
and I do not know what to do.

I cry to You, Lord.
Save my life!
It is the devil who surrounds me.
He has hooked me and pulls and pulls.
And I?
Lord, You are silent.
The silence of You...
I struggle
amid a thousand anguishes of love
and your absence...

496. *How I would like to love You,*
Jesus, Lord, my God!
And here you have me in a feeling
full of contradictions.
I do not feel You.
Where are You?
Come, for I will die!
I cannot take it.
The devil invites me to sin,
to escape from being in You...
If you are not already gone...
Temptations of my soul,
temptations.
It moves me to think
that You made yourself the last,
wretched, sin,
My God.
What a mystery!

> *If God has made himself sin for me,*[466]
> *What can I say…?*

497. *And in this occurrence,*
      in this being in You,
      Oh! What suffering,
      What pain…
      Where are You taking me?
      Or they are taking me…
      What a mystery is my life.
      It is the mystery of You,
      of me, and of the others.

498. *And in this being of You and of things,*
      and in this endlessness of mournful sighs,
      of the howling of those street dogs.
      And things are calm.
      Unmoved, they accompany us…
      in the silence of time
      that passes and caresses them.

499. *I would like to be, crying,*
      your soul's companion,
      my Jesus,
      a wounded deer that,
      lost in the dark forest,
      finds no consolation.
      Deer that thirsts,
      wounded deer.

---

[466] Cf. 2 Cor 5:21.

500. *And living and living*
in the constant remembrance of You.
In this endlessness of instants
that never cease,
with my wounded heart.

501. And in this extreme weakness in which I find myself, what can I do? At night, the devil wants to suffocate me, and You, don't leave me, Lord. My soul is raw and I am suffering so much. What has happened to me that I am a martyred soul, constantly groaning? Lord, have mercy. It's as if I took my soul in my hands, and I feel it beating and trembling while it groans. Where are we going, my soul? Enter within me and rest.

502. O my Jesus! Why is my living so pressed? I feel enclosed in a strong embrace… Is it you squeezing me, embracing me so tightly…? How hard it is to live always groaning. Why is my life a suffering in You? I go around horrified at myself. Oh, what pain! You, You alone, and my poor soul… My heart is weakened by so many sufferings. The doctor tells me I shouldn't suffer, and I… Living… What a mystery existence is. Who am I? Where am I going? And things continue on impassively. And time continues to pass. I go and just the thought that I will find myself before You… What can I say? Do not take me to Hell. I understand that life is an endlessness of incommensurable glory. And I? And mankind? What is man? You made him great, great,

to the point of having the ability to kill you: free, free. He broke the tablets and fell into Hell... And You there, on that hill, crucified...

503. *And in this unpleasantness of impassive things,*
and in this being in which my soul has left.
Where are you, oh my soul?
Here am I, broken, groaning,
in the instants of inexorable time...
And where are you?
Do not let me go
toward the nothingness of my things.

504. *My soul is immersed*
among folds and duplicities, among the fabrics
of life, interwoven with
worries, anguishes and sins...
They would like to sew my soul to
lies...
And in my anguish, I cried out
to the Lord and he helped me. I don't know
how I came out. Here I am! In this
green meadow. For I died yesterday.
Empty hospitals, with dirty
rooms, timid you were, my soul.
Trembling... and in my anguish
I cried out to the Lord, and here I am
in this meadow full of light
with my soul that expands
with joy, full of a new peace
never felt before.

> *The thing is: yesterday they held my funeral*
> *And I saw them.*

505. Lord, Lord! How will I go on? Carmen, they tell me she's dying, poor thing, how much the Way owes Carmen! What a wonderful woman, with a masterful genius of freedom and love for the Church! She never flattered me, always after me. She told me the truth. The youth, above all the girls, adored her. She always said that the woman is the most important thing in the Church and in the world because she carries inside her being the factory of life. And she would say, "Do not trust men," and "You can have Kiko…" But she was always at my side to help me. What a mystery people are, their personality! Carmen, what a mystery! One day she said to me, "I pass for a crazy woman in the Vatican, so that everyone will say, 'Kiko is a saint to put up with this woman!'"

506. *Why are you crying, my soul?*
Why are you crying?
Carmen has gone with the Lord.
Yes! I feel her love
close to my heart.
What an extraordinary woman!
How much she loved me![467]

---

[467] These last two numbers were written in 2016 and are included at the author's request in memory of Carmen, who died July 19, 2016 (Editor's note).

AFTERWORD

by Ricardo Blázquez Perez
Cardinal Archbishop of Valladolid
President of the Spanish Episcopal Conference

The Neocatechumenal Way has its roots in the Second Vatican Council. It is a vigorous charism, universally extended and rich in fruits of personal conversion and renewal of the Church. Kiko Argüello and Carmen Hernandez are its initiators. It was born among the poor in Palomeras Altas in Madrid, and its place of origin has branded it with the seal of the evangelization of the poor, the sinners, and those discarded in life. The book we now present shows the same characteristics. Although the author doubted whether it was appropriate to publish it for fear of vanity (No. 451), I am convinced that he was correct in overcoming this uncertainty, to diffuse, in this way, too, the charism received from the Spirit of God destined for the service of others.

This book is a collection of aphorisms that can be read in any order. They are reflections stemming from an event, a convivence or an encounter; spiritual wake-up calls either announcing or denouncing; questions or calls to hope that the reader feels are for him: sometimes daring confidences that spring from the author's soul; occasionally, they take the form of a hymn or a psalm, full of ardent pleas and fervent thanksgiving to God.

From the data contained in the little passages, one can somewhat follow the historical thread from 1988 to 2014. The passages are united by the history of faith of the author and of the Neocatechumenal Way more than by any thematic development, although many references to this specific charism are dispersed throughout.

It is a history full of joy and suffering; it illuminates the author's struggle to fulfill faithfully the commission received from God. The destinies of the Way and its initiators are inseparably linked in the trials and joys described herein. The ways humility appears in its various nuances is striking. It shows the contrast between the magnitude of the evangelizing charism that is the Neocatechumenal Way and the awareness of weakness and sin possessed by the personal instrument chosen by God.

Normally, fear precedes a difficult convivence, a meeting, a trip, a visit; and thanksgiving follows the victorious action of the Lord. The author is conscious that if God did not intervene, it would be a failure because there is a radical imbalance between the personal instrument, that is always deficient, and God's promise. The author highlights his overwhelming fragility and the Lord's truly amazing work. His surprise at the action of God in a thousand places and a thousand celebrations is preceded by the sincere conviction of his own weakness, of his trust in God, whom he entreats with loud cries on occasion, and the exultant thanksgiving that will follow. These thoughts read in a leisurely manner and meditated upon for an appropriate time can lead us to thought, prayer, admiration, and self-questioning.

Many books of a literary genre similar to that which the reader has before him have emerged throughout the history of the Church. We can remember in an already distant past St. John of the Cross' *Sayings of Light and Love* or Pascal's *Thoughts*. In the twentieth century, I have had the opportunity to encounter others. The most famous is most likely *The Way* by St. Josemaria Escrivá, published for the first time in Valencia in 1939. In Avila, I read the book *Priestly Suggestions*, published by the rector of that seminary, Don Baldomero Jimenez Duque, in 1962; Josemaria Javierre compiled the thoughts of St. Angela de la Cruz with the title, *A Treasure in an Earthen Vessel*, which appeared in print in 1997. Since this type of book is not ordinarily systematically arranged by theme or subject matter, it is neither necessary nor recommended to read them in order. Each number is like a sip to be savored slowly.

In order to understand the 506 numbers comprising this book called *Annotations* more easily, it may help to have some knowledge of the most salient features of the author and the Neocatechumenal Way. I will continue with a few brushstrokes.

The evangelization in our time, the "new evangelization," Christian initiation, and the catechumenate, rooted in the Second Vatican Council, have unfolded in a profound and original manner in the Neocatechumenal Way. The catechumenate is currently, like in the ancient Church, the means of evangelization, personal conversion, and formation of the Christian community. This framework facilitates the understanding of this book.

The repeated experiences of people in thousands of communities validates the fact that in the measure in which the catechumenal itinerary advances, a living and powerful symbiosis occurs between personal and ecclesial faith. The feeling of Church based on community life is born within the participants. Being part of the Church does not remain a membership somewhat external to the person, but, rather is internalized in an experience that is born from, and grows with, the journey.

Experience validates that in the Neocatechumenal Way the fundamental realities of the Church are wholly transmitted and personally assimilated: the Creed, the Commandments of God in the spirit of the Sermon on the Mount, the praying of the Our Father and the Psalms, the sacramental celebrations of the Church, above all Baptism, Eucharist and Penance. The constant proclamation of the *kerygma* leads to, refreshes, and solidifies faith. It is a post-baptismal catechumenate, "neocatechumenate," since the majority of the community members have already been baptized.

With the celebration of the Liturgy in the vernacular, the poor biblical formation of Christians was made more evident. In the Neocatechumenal Way, the proclamation of the Word of God and the celebration of the Eucharist reinforce each other. An authentic evangelization requires that the Word of God, the sacraments, and the concrete existence of the people be vitally united.

Within the Church, which literally means "convocation" of God and is the "homeland" of every vocation, each catechumen discovers the vocation to which God calls him: to Christian marriage, to the priestly ministry, to the contemplative or apostolic religious life, to be an itinerant catechist, to form part of a mission family. The Neocatechumenal Way is enormously fertile in priestly and religious vocations without seeing them as a specific end. How many marriages and families have been rebuilt through the Gospel heard in the communities! How effective the transmission of Christian faith to the children is in these families!

The apostolic dimension of faith and the missionary zeal of the participants in community are worthy of emphasis. It is natural that this occurs because the Christian vocation is by nature missionary. Several basic Christian attitudes are commonly found in the Neocatechumenal Way and these appear in this book as a reflection of this deep reality. The love for Jesus Christ who died for our sins and has given us eternal life by his resurrection; the conviction that mankind needs to be saved and that in spite of all appearances, we clamor for this salvation offered freely by God in Jesus Christ, died and risen; the trust in the providence of the heavenly Father who cares for his children; humble love as a breeding ground for reconciliation inside and outside of the community; the evangelical conviction, reinforced by experience, that neither money, nor pleasure, nor power can save. Idols do not save but destroy. Only in the glorious cross of Jesus Christ does God offer salvation through the foolishness of the preaching; our heart is opened through prayer to receive the grace of God.

Each of the numbers in this book is a deposit and reflection of the artistic talent and existential experience of the author; the characteristics of the Neocatechumenal Way can be seen on each page. Of course, for those who are familiar with the Way they are extraordinarily eloquent, but anyone can perceive the human and Christian vigor that permeates them. We hope that this book will be reach a broad audience and that it may be an effective aid to evangelization.

TABLE OF CONTENTS

FOREWORD 9
PREFACE 13
INTRODUCTION 17
ANNOTATIONS 1988-2014 19
AFTERWORD 267
TABLE OF CONTENTS 272

www.ingramcontent.com/pod-product-compliance
Lightning Source LLC
Chambersburg PA
CBHW031947080426
42735CB00007B/293